C Programming

© 2025 Mark John Lado

Mastering C Programming

From Basics to Advanced Concepts

MARK JOHN LADO

No part of this publication may be reproduced, distributed, or transmitted in any form or by any means, including photocopying, recording, or other electronic or mechanical methods, without the prior written permission of the author, except in the case of brief quotations embodied in critical reviews and certain other noncommercial uses permitted by copyright law.

All trademarks, service marks, trade names, logos, and icons (collectively, "Marks") appearing in this publication are the property of their respective owners. This publication may contain references to various Marks for informational and illustrative purposes only. The use of such Marks herein does not constitute or imply any endorsement or sponsorship by the respective owners of those Marks, nor does it grant any license, express or implied, to use any Marks. Any unauthorized use of any Marks is strictly prohibited.

Copyright © 2025 Mark John Lado. All rights reserved.

ISBN: 9798311099943

www.markjohnlado.com

DEDICATION

To the aspiring computer technologists and dedicated educators who embark on the rewarding journey of mastering C programming. This book is dedicated to your curiosity, perseverance, and passion for the foundational principles that underpin the digital world. May this exploration of C programming empower you to not only understand the inner workings of computing but also to build innovative and robust solutions that shape the future.

To the students, may C programming be your stepping stone to profound understanding and boundless creation.

To the educators, thank you for illuminating the path for generations to come. May this resource serve as a valuable companion in your shared pursuit of knowledge and excellence in computer technology.

Let the power and elegance of C programming inspire you to write code that is not only functional but also impactful and enduring.

© 2025 Mark John Lado

ACKNOWLEDGMENTS

This book is a culmination of dedicated effort, and its creation would not have been possible without the support and inspiration of numerous individuals and resources. I extend my sincere gratitude to the educators and mentors who have instilled in me a deep appreciation for computer science and the elegance of C programming. Their guidance and insights have been invaluable in shaping my understanding and approach to teaching these fundamental concepts. I also acknowledge the countless students who, through their questions and enthusiasm, have continually refined my perspective and motivated the clarity and depth of this work. Finally, heartfelt thanks go to the authors and researchers whose cited works have provided a solid foundation of knowledge and credibility to this exploration of C programming. Their contributions are deeply appreciated.

Table of Contents

Chapter 1 Introduction to C Programming

In this chapter, you will learn the following:

1. Overview of C Programming
2. History and Evolution of C
3. Features of C
4. Installing and Setting Up a C Compiler

Laying the Foundation for Computational Mastery

The journey into the world of programming often begins with a fundamental question: why choose C? In an era dominated by high-level languages and specialized scripting tools, C's enduring relevance might seem paradoxical to the uninitiated. However, a closer examination reveals that C remains a cornerstone of modern computing, a language whose influence permeates virtually every layer of the technological landscape. From the operating systems that power our computers and smartphones, such as Linux, macOS, and Windows kernels, to the firmware embedded within microcontrollers governing countless devices, C's efficiency, control, and portability make it an unparalleled choice for performance-critical applications. Consider the vast infrastructure of the internet itself, where core networking protocols and server software frequently leverage C for its speed and ability to interact directly with system hardware. Furthermore, in fields like game development, high-performance computing, and embedded systems design, C is not merely a viable option; it is often the *de facto* standard. Understanding C, therefore, is not just learning a programming language; it's gaining a profound understanding of how computers function at a fundamental level, equipping learners with a versatile toolset applicable across a diverse spectrum of computational challenges. This chapter will embark on this learning journey by exploring the bedrock principles of C programming, setting the stage for mastering its intricacies in subsequent chapters.

To truly appreciate C's position in the programming world, it's essential to understand its historical context and evolutionary path. C emerged from the legendary Bell Laboratories in the late 1960s and early 1970s, conceived by Dennis Ritchie as an evolution of earlier languages like BCPL and B. Its primary motivation was to develop a portable operating system, which culminated in the creation of Unix – an operating system that itself revolutionized computing by being written almost entirely in C. This symbiotic relationship between language and operating system was instrumental in C's early adoption and growth. As Tanenbaum and Woodhull meticulously documented in their analysis of operating systems (Tanenbaum & Woodhull, 2006), Unix's success significantly propelled C into the academic and commercial spheres, leading to widespread adoption beyond Bell Labs. The standardization of C by ANSI in 1989 (ANSI C or C89) and subsequently by ISO (ISO C90, C99, C11, and beyond) further solidified its position, ensuring portability and consistency across different platforms and compilers. This standardization process, as detailed by Harbison and Steele in their comprehensive C reference manual (Harbison & Steele, 2002), has been crucial in maintaining C's long-term viability and enabling its evolution while preserving backward compatibility – a testament to its well-designed core and the foresight of its creators.

The enduring appeal of C stems from a constellation of powerful features that cater to both low-level system programming and high-level application development. Foremost amongst these is its exceptional portability. Code written in standard C can be compiled and run on virtually any platform with a C compiler, a feat rarely matched by other languages with similar capabilities. This "write once, compile anywhere" philosophy, while not entirely without platform-specific nuances, significantly reduces development effort and fosters code reusability.

Furthermore, C is renowned for its efficiency and performance. As Ritchie himself articulated in his seminal work on the language (Ritchie, 1993), C was designed to be close to the machine, allowing programmers to exert fine-grained control over hardware resources and memory management. This characteristic makes C ideally suited for resource-constrained environments and performance-critical applications where every cycle counts. Its flexibility is equally noteworthy. C seamlessly blends high-level programming constructs with low-level access, enabling developers to work at different levels of abstraction as needed. This spectrum of capabilities extends from crafting device drivers and operating system kernels to building complex application software and embedded systems. Moreover, C's modular design, facilitated by functions and libraries, promotes code organization and reusability, contributing to maintainable and scalable software projects. These features collectively underscore why C remains a vital tool in the contemporary programmer's arsenal.

Before embarking on writing C programs, a crucial initial step is setting up the development environment. This primarily involves installing and configuring a C compiler on your system. For beginners, a readily accessible and widely used compiler is GCC (GNU Compiler Collection), particularly prevalent on Linux and macOS systems. On Windows, MinGW (Minimalist GNU for Windows) provides a GCC environment, and Microsoft Visual C++ (MSVC) is another powerful, commercially supported option. To verify if GCC is already installed on a Linux or macOS system, open a terminal and type `gcc --version`. If GCC is installed, version information will be displayed. If not, package managers like `apt` (on Debian/Ubuntu), `yum` (on Fedora/CentOS), or brew (on macOS with Homebrew) can be utilized to install GCC. For instance, on Ubuntu, the command sudo apt-get update && sudo apt-get install gcc will install GCC and essential build tools. On Windows using MinGW, download the installer from the MinGW website and follow the on-screen instructions, ensuring to add the MinGW bin directory to your system's PATH environment variable. This allows the operating system to locate the compiler executable from any command prompt. Similarly, for MSVC, installing Visual Studio Community Edition will include the necessary C++ build tools, including the C compiler. After installation, verifying the setup is essential. Open a terminal or command prompt and type gcc --version (or cl for MSVC) again. A successful installation will be confirmed by the compiler version output, signifying that the development environment is ready for your first C program. In the subsequent chapter, we will delve into the structure of a C program and take the first exciting steps in writing and executing code.

Chapter 2 Writing Your First C Program

In this chapter, you will learn the following:

1. Structure of a C Program
2. Compiling and Running a C Program
3. Understanding the main() Function
4. Comments in C

Embarking on Your C Programming Journey - From Structure to Execution

The initial foray into any programming language is often marked by the creation of the canonical "Hello, World!" program. This seemingly simple exercise is profoundly important, as it encapsulates the fundamental steps involved in writing, compiling, and executing code in a new environment. In C, this rite of passage provides a tangible introduction to the structural elements that constitute a C program and demystifies the process of transforming human-readable code into machine-executable instructions. Understanding the anatomy of even the simplest C program lays the groundwork for tackling more complex coding challenges in subsequent stages of learning. This chapter will meticulously dissect the structure of a C program, guide you through the compilation and execution process, illuminate the crucial role of the main() function, and emphasize the importance of comments for code clarity and maintainability. Mastering these foundational concepts is not merely about getting your first program to run; it's about developing a robust understanding of the C programming workflow and establishing good coding habits from the outset.

Every C program, regardless of its complexity, adheres to a fundamental structural template. At its core, a typical C program comprises several key components working in concert. Firstly, preprocessor directives, often starting with a # symbol, instruct the C preprocessor to perform actions *before* the actual compilation begins. A ubiquitous example is #include <stdio.h>, which directs the preprocessor to include the standard input/output library header file, providing access to functions like printf() for displaying output. As Kernighan and Ritchie, the creators of C, aptly demonstrate in "The C Programming Language" (Kernighan & Ritchie, 1988), header files serve as essential interfaces, declaring functions and data structures that are defined elsewhere, often in system libraries. Following preprocessor directives, the heart of every C program is the main() function. This function is the designated entry point where program execution commences. Its structure typically follows the form int main() { /* program statements */ return 0; }. The curly braces {} delimit the body of the main() function, enclosing a sequence of statements that constitute the program's logic. Within the main() function, statements are instructions that the computer will execute sequentially. These can range from simple operations like variable assignments to complex control flow structures and function calls. Finally, the return 0; statement within main() signifies successful program termination to the operating system. While seemingly minimal, understanding this basic structure is paramount, as it forms the blueprint for all C programs, providing a framework for organizing code and defining program behavior (Deitel & Deitel, 2015).

Once a C program is written, it must undergo a transformation process to become executable by a computer. This process is known as compilation, and in C, it typically involves several distinct stages. Initially, the preprocessor handles directives like #include and #define, expanding macros and incorporating header files into the source code. Next, the compiler translates the preprocessed C code into assembly language – a low-level language that is closer to machine code but still human-readable. The assembler then converts the assembly code into object code, which is in binary format but may contain unresolved references to external functions and libraries. Finally, the linker resolves these external references by combining the object code with necessary library code, producing the final executable file. To illustrate this practically, consider the classic "Hello, World!" program:

```
#include <stdio.h>


int main() {
    printf("Hello, World!\n");
    return 0;
}
```

To compile this program using GCC on a Linux or macOS system, you would typically open a terminal, navigate to the directory containing the source file (let's assume it's named `hello.c`), and execute the command `gcc hello.c -o hello`. Here, `gcc` is the compiler invocation, `hello.c` is the source file, and `-o hello` specifies that the output executable file should be named `hello`. Upon successful compilation, an executable file named `hello` will be created in the same directory. To run this program, you would then execute `./hello` in the terminal. The output "Hello, World!" followed by a newline character will be displayed on the console. Common challenges at this stage often involve syntax errors in the code (misspellings, missing semicolons, etc.). The compiler is your first line of defense against these errors; carefully reviewing compiler error messages is crucial for debugging. Error messages often indicate the line number and type of error, providing valuable clues for correction. For instance, a "syntax error: expected ';' before 'return'" message clearly points to a missing semicolon at the end of the preceding statement. Practicing compiling and running simple programs, and meticulously addressing compiler errors, builds essential debugging skills early in the learning process.

The main() function, as previously mentioned, serves as the starting point of program execution. Its declaration int main() warrants closer scrutiny. The int keyword specifies that the main() function is expected to return an integer value to the operating system upon completion. Conventionally, a return value of 0 signifies successful program execution, while any non-zero value typically indicates an error or abnormal termination. This return value allows the operating system or calling programs to assess the execution status of the C program. While int main() is the most common form, you might also encounter int main(void) and int main(int argc, char *argv[]). int main(void) explicitly indicates that the main() function does not accept any command-line arguments. int main(int argc, char *argv[]) is used when the program needs to process command-line arguments passed to it when it is executed. argc (argument count) is an integer representing the number of command-line arguments, and argv (argument vector) is an array of strings, where each string is a command-line argument. Understanding the main() function is fundamental because it defines the program's entry point and controls the overall flow of execution. Incorrectly defining or misunderstanding the role of main() can lead to program execution failures or unexpected behavior (Prata, 2014).

Finally, comments, often overlooked by novice programmers, are an indispensable aspect of writing effective and maintainable C code. Comments are explanatory notes embedded within the source code that are ignored by the compiler but are invaluable for human readers. C supports two types of comments: single-line comments, initiated by //, which comment out everything to the end of the line, and multi-line comments, enclosed within /* and */, which can span multiple lines.

Effective commenting is not about stating the obvious (e.g., i++; // increment i); rather, it's about explaining the *why* behind the code – the purpose, logic, and design decisions. For instance, in a complex function, comments can clarify the algorithm being implemented, the assumptions made, or the intended behavior under specific conditions. As McConnell emphasizes in "Code Complete" (McConnell, 2004), well-placed comments significantly enhance code readability and maintainability, especially in collaborative projects and when revisiting code after a period of time. Imagine revisiting the "Hello, World!" program after several months; adding comments like // Program to print "Hello, World!" to the console and // Include standard input/output library for printf() would immediately remind you of the program's purpose and dependencies. Consistent use of clear, concise, and informative comments is a hallmark of professional programming practice and becomes increasingly crucial as program complexity grows. By embracing comments from the start, you cultivate a habit of writing self-documenting code, which will prove invaluable throughout your programming journey.

© 2025 Mark John Lado

Chapter 3 C Language Fundamentals

In this chapter, you will learn the following:

1. C Tokens
    a. Keywords
    b. Identifiers
    c. Constants
    d. Strings
    e. Special Symbols
2. Displaying Text - Escape Codes

The Lexical Building Blocks of Code

Just as sentences are composed of words, and words of letters, C programs are built from fundamental lexical units known as *tokens.* Understanding C tokens is akin to learning the alphabet and vocabulary of the language. These tokens are the smallest individual units recognized by the C compiler and form the basic building blocks for constructing statements, expressions, and ultimately, entire programs. Mastering these fundamental elements is crucial for any aspiring C programmer, as they dictate the syntax and structure of valid C code. This chapter will delve into the various categories of C tokens, exploring keywords, identifiers, constants, strings, and special symbols, and will further illuminate the essential concept of escape codes for controlling text display, providing a solid foundation for writing meaningful and well-formatted C programs. Grasping these seemingly atomic components is the first step towards fluency in C, enabling the construction of robust and expressive computational solutions.

C tokens are broadly categorized into several distinct types, each serving a specific purpose in the language's syntax. *Keywords* are reserved words that have predefined meanings in C and cannot be used as identifiers. Examples include int, float, while, for, if, else, return, and struct. These keywords form the core grammar of C, controlling program flow, defining data types, and structuring program logic. As Deitel and Deitel explain in "C: How to Program" (Deitel & Deitel, 2015), keywords are the vocabulary of the C language, and understanding their precise function is vital for writing syntactically correct code. Attempting to use a keyword as a variable name, for instance, will result in a compilation error, highlighting their reserved status. *Identifiers*, on the other hand, are names given to variables, functions, arrays, structures, and other user-defined entities. They are user-defined tokens used to refer to these program elements. Identifiers must adhere to specific naming rules: they must begin with a letter or underscore (_), followed by letters, digits, or underscores. They are also case-sensitive, meaning variableName and variablename are treated as distinct identifiers. Choosing meaningful identifiers is a cornerstone of good programming practice, making code more readable and self-documenting. For example, using student_age instead of a cryptic name like sa clearly conveys the variable's purpose.

Constants represent fixed values that do not change during program execution. C supports various types of constants, including integer constants (e.g., 10, -5, 0), floating-point constants (e.g., 3.14, -2.5, 0.0), character constants (e.g., 'A', '9', '*'), and string literals (discussed separately below). Integer constants can be expressed in decimal, octal (prefixed with 0), or hexadecimal (prefixed with 0x). Floating-point constants can be written in standard decimal notation or exponential notation (e.g., 1.23e-4). Character constants are enclosed in single quotes and represent single characters. Constants are essential for representing fixed data values within a program, such as mathematical constants, limits, or configuration parameters. As Kernighan and Ritchie illustrate in "The C Programming Language" (Kernighan & Ritchie, 1988), constants provide a way to embed literal values directly into the source code. *String literals*, often simply referred to as "strings," are sequences of characters enclosed in double quotes (e.g., "Hello, World!", "C Programming"). Unlike character constants which represent single characters, strings represent sequences of characters and are treated as arrays of characters terminated by a null character (\0). Strings are fundamental for representing textual data in C programs, used for messages, labels, file names, and various other text-based operations. Finally, *special symbols* are tokens that have specific grammatical or syntactical meanings in C. These include punctuation marks like semicolons (;), commas (,), parentheses (), curly braces {}, square brackets [], and operators like +, -, *, /, =, ==, &&, ||, and many others. These symbols structure C code, delimit statements, define code blocks, and perform operations. Understanding the role of each special symbol is critical for writing syntactically correct and semantically meaningful C programs.

Beyond these core token categories, mastering the display of text output is crucial for creating user-interactive programs and providing informative feedback. The printf() function from the <stdio.h> library is the primary tool for displaying text in C. However, simply placing text within double quotes is often insufficient to achieve desired formatting. *Escape codes* are special character sequences that begin with a backslash \ and are used within strings to represent non-printable characters or control the output format. The most commonly used escape code is \n, the newline character. When \n is encountered in a string passed to printf(), it inserts a newline character, causing subsequent output to begin on the next line. Other essential escape codes include \t for horizontal tab, \r for carriage return, \\ to display a literal backslash, \" to display a literal double quote, and \' to display a literal single quote. Let's illustrate the use of escape codes with a practical example:

```
#include <stdio.h>

int main() {
    printf("This is line 1.\n");
    printf("This is line 2.\n");
    printf("Column 1\tColumn 2\tColumn 3\n");
    printf("To print a backslash, use \\\\.\n");
    printf("To print quotes, use \\\" and \\'.\n");
    return 0;
}
```

In this code, the first two `printf()` statements use `\n` to print "This is line 1." and "This is line 2." on separate lines. The third `printf()` uses `\t` to create tab-separated columns "Column 1", "Column 2", and "Column 3". The fourth and fifth `printf()` statements demonstrate how to print literal backslashes and quotes using `\\`, `\"`, and `\'` respectively. Compiling and running this code will showcase the effect of these escape codes on the formatted text output. As Prata emphasizes in "C Primer Plus" (Prata, 2014), escape codes are indispensable for achieving precise control over text formatting in C output, allowing for the creation of well-structured and readable program output for users and log files alike. Understanding and effectively utilizing C tokens and escape codes is not just about syntax; it's about gaining control over the fundamental building blocks of C programs, empowering programmers to express complex logic and communicate effectively with both the computer and human readers of their code.

Chapter 4 Data Types and Variables

In this chapter, you will learn the following:

1. Primitive Data Types
2. Type Modifiers (signed, unsigned, short, long)
3. Variables
    a. Declaring and Initializing Variables
    b. Constants (#define and const)
4. Formatted Input and Output
5. Using printf() and scanf()

The Cornerstones of Data Manipulation in C

In the realm of programming, data is the lifeblood of any application. Whether it's numerical values representing sensor readings in an embedded system, textual information in a word processor, or complex structures defining network packets, programs are fundamentally concerned with processing and manipulating data. C, being a language that prioritizes efficiency and control, provides a robust system of *data types* and *variables* to effectively manage this data. Understanding data types and variables is not just about adhering to C syntax; it's about learning how to represent information accurately and efficiently within a computer's memory, a skill paramount for developing any meaningful C program. This chapter will meticulously explore the primitive data types offered by C, delve into type modifiers for fine-grained control over data representation, elucidate the concepts of variables – their declaration, initialization, and the distinction between variables and constants – and finally, introduce formatted input and output operations using the essential `printf()` and `scanf()` functions. Mastering these concepts is crucial because they form the foundation upon which all data processing and manipulation in C programs are built.

C offers a set of *primitive data types* that are the fundamental building blocks for representing various kinds of data. These types are built into the language and directly supported by most processors, ensuring efficiency and portability. The most common primitive types are integers, floating-point numbers, and characters. *Integers* are whole numbers without fractional parts, represented by the `int` keyword. Integers are used for counting, indexing, representing discrete quantities, and various control variables within programs. For instance, in a real-world application like an embedded system controlling a motor, integer variables might track the number of rotations, steps taken, or sensor readings. *Floating-point numbers*, used for representing numbers with fractional parts or very large or very small numbers, are represented by the float and double keywords. float provides single-precision floating-point numbers, while double offers double-precision, providing greater accuracy but potentially requiring more memory. In scientific simulations, engineering calculations, or financial applications, floating-point numbers are indispensable for representing measurements, calculated values, and quantities that require fractional precision. Consider a program simulating weather patterns; floating-point variables would be used to represent temperature, pressure, wind speed, and humidity. *Characters*, represented by the char keyword, are used to store single characters, such as letters, digits, and symbols. Characters are essential for text processing, string manipulation, and representing individual elements of textual data. In a text editor application, character variables would be used to store and manipulate individual characters of the text being edited. Finally, the void type, while not strictly a data type in the same sense, is a special type that signifies the absence of a value. It is primarily used to specify that a function does not return a value or as a generic pointer type (which will be discussed in later chapters). Understanding the nuances of each primitive data type is crucial for choosing the appropriate type to represent different kinds of data accurately and efficiently in C programs (Koenig, 1994).

To provide even finer control over data representation, C offers *type modifiers*. These modifiers can be applied to the basic integer and floating-point types to alter their size, range, and interpretation. The common type modifiers are signed, unsigned, short, and long. signed and unsigned modifiers apply to integer types (int and char). signed (which is the default for int and char) indicates that the variable can represent both positive and negative values. unsigned, conversely, restricts the variable to non-negative values (zero and positive), effectively doubling the range of positive values that can be stored for a given number of bits. In scenarios where negative values are not needed and maximizing the positive range is critical, such as representing memory addresses or counters that only increment, unsigned types can be beneficial. short and long modifiers also apply to integer types, and long can also apply to double. short int (often abbreviated as short) typically reduces the memory allocated to an integer, potentially saving space when dealing with a large number of small integer values. long int (often abbreviated as long) and long long int (or long long, introduced in C99 standard) increase the memory allocated to an integer, allowing for representation of a wider range of integer values, essential for applications dealing with very large or very small integers. Similarly, long double provides extended precision for floating-point numbers, useful in scientific and financial calculations where high accuracy is paramount. Choosing the correct type modifier is a trade-off between memory usage and the range of values needed. Careful consideration of these factors can lead to more efficient and resource-conscious C programs (Puntambekar, 2008).

Variables are named storage locations in memory that can hold data values of a specific type. They are the fundamental entities through which programs manipulate data. Before a variable can be used, it must be *declared*. Declaration associates a name (identifier) with a specific data type. The syntax for declaring a variable is data_type variable_name;. For example, int age; declares a variable named age of type int. A variable can also be *initialized* at the time of declaration, assigning it an initial value. Initialization can be done at declaration itself using the syntax data_type variable_name = initial_value;. For instance, int count = 0; declares an integer variable count and initializes it to 0. While declaration merely reserves memory, initialization assigns a meaningful starting value. It is good programming practice to initialize variables upon declaration to avoid undefined behavior and improve code readability. Variable names (identifiers) must follow the rules discussed in the previous chapter, starting with a letter or underscore and containing letters, digits, or underscores, and are case-sensitive. Choosing descriptive variable names that clearly indicate their purpose is crucial for code maintainability and understandability. In contrast to variables, *constants* represent values that are fixed and cannot be changed during program execution. C provides two primary ways to define constants: using the #define preprocessor directive and the const keyword. #define creates symbolic constants by instructing the preprocessor to perform text substitution before compilation. For example, #define PI 3.14159 replaces every occurrence of PI in the code with 3.14159 before compilation. const keyword, on the other hand, declares a variable as read-only. For example, const float gravity = 9.8; declares gravity as a constant float variable with a value of 9.8. While both methods define constants, const constants are type-safe and checked by the compiler, offering better type safety and scope control compared to #define constants which are simple text substitutions and lack type checking (King, 2008).

Finally, to interact with the user and display program results, C provides *formatted input and output* capabilities through functions like printf() and scanf() from the <stdio.h> library. printf() is used for formatted output, displaying values of variables and text to the console. Its syntax is printf("format string", argument1, argument2, ...);. The "format string" contains placeholders called *format specifiers* that indicate the type of data to be printed and how it should be formatted. Common format specifiers include %d for integers, %f for floating-point numbers, %c for characters, and %s for strings. For example, printf("The age is: %d\n", age); will print "The age is: " followed by the value of the integer variable age and a newline character. scanf() is used for formatted input, reading data from the user's input (typically from the keyboard) and storing it in variables. Its syntax is scanf("format string", &variable1, &variable2, ...);. The "format string" in scanf() also uses format specifiers to indicate the expected data type to be read. Crucially, scanf() requires the address-of operator & before variable names, as it needs to know the memory location where the input value should be stored. For example, scanf("%d", &age); will read an integer value from the user and store it in the age variable. Let's illustrate formatted input and output with an example:

```
#include <stdio.h>

int main() {
    int number;
    float price;

    printf("Enter an integer and a price: ");
    scanf("%d %f", &number, &price);

    printf("You entered: Number = %d, Price = %.2f\n", number, price);
```

```
    return 0;
}
```

In this code, the program prompts the user to enter an integer and a price. scanf("%d %f", &number, &price); reads an integer and a float value from the input and stores them in number and price respectively. printf("You entered: Number = %d, Price = %.2f\n", number, price); then displays the entered values, formatting the price to two decimal places using %.2f. A common challenge with scanf() is *buffer overflow*, which occurs when the input exceeds the allocated buffer size, potentially leading to security vulnerabilities. Therefore, using scanf() directly for unbounded string input should be approached with caution, and safer alternatives like fgets() for string input and input validation techniques are often recommended in production code. Mastering data types, variables, constants, and formatted input/output is foundational for building interactive and data-driven C programs, enabling programs to receive input, process data, and present results effectively to the user (Hanly & Koffman, 2009).

© 2025 Mark John Lado

Chapter 5 Operators in C

In this chapter, you will learn the following:

1. Assignment Operators
2. Arithmetic Operators
    a. Increment (++) and Decrement (--)
    b. Operator Precedence and Associativity
3. Relational and Logical Operators
    a. Precedence of Relational and Logical Operators
4. Bitwise Operators

The Engine of Computation

Operators are the workhorses of any programming language, and C is no exception. They are the symbols that instruct the compiler to perform specific operations on data, ranging from simple arithmetic calculations to complex logical evaluations and bit-level manipulations. A deep understanding of operators is not just about memorizing symbols; it is about grasping the fundamental mechanisms by which programs transform and process data to achieve desired outcomes. In essence, operators are the verbs of the programming language, dictating the actions performed on the nouns (operands – variables and constants). This chapter will meticulously dissect the various categories of operators in C, including assignment, arithmetic, relational, logical, and bitwise operators, paying close attention to operator precedence, associativity, and real-world applications, thereby equipping learners with the tools to construct powerful and expressive C programs. Mastering operators is not merely about syntax; it is about gaining control over the computational engine of C, enabling the implementation of intricate algorithms and solutions.

The simplest yet most fundamental operator is the *assignment operator* (`=`). It is used to assign a value to a variable. In C, assignment is an expression, and the value of the assignment expression is the value assigned. This characteristic allows for chained assignments like `a = b = c = 10;`, where the value `10` is assigned to `c`, then to `b`, and finally to `a`. Beyond simple assignment, C provides a suite of *compound assignment operators* that combine an arithmetic operation with assignment. These include `+=`, `-=`, `*=`, `/=`, `%=`, `&=`, `|=`, `^=`, `<<=`, and `>>=`. For example, `x += 5;` is equivalent to `x = x + 5;`, providing a more concise way to increment a variable by 5. Similarly, y *= 2; is equivalent to y = y * 2;, doubling the value of y. These compound operators not only enhance code readability but can also, in some compiler implementations, lead to slightly more efficient code execution. Consider a real-world scenario in financial software: calculating compound interest repeatedly updates an account balance. Using compound assignment operators like balance *= (1 + interest_rate); elegantly updates the balance variable with each compounding period, reflecting the accumulated interest. As Schildt notes in "C: The Complete Reference" (Schildt, 2000), compound assignment operators contribute to writing cleaner and more efficient C code, especially when dealing with iterative calculations or value updates within loops.

Arithmetic operators perform mathematical computations. C provides the standard arithmetic operators: addition (+), subtraction (-), multiplication (*), division (/), and modulus (%). Integer division truncates towards zero, meaning 5 / 2 results in 2. The modulus operator % yields the remainder of integer division; 5 % 2 results in 1. In practical applications, arithmetic operators are ubiquitous, from simple calculations in calculators to complex simulations in scientific computing. Consider a program simulating projectile motion: arithmetic operators would be used extensively to calculate velocity, acceleration, distance, and trajectory based on physical formulas. Furthermore, C provides the *increment operator* (++) and *decrement operator* (--). These operators are unique in that they modify the value of a variable directly. Both operators have prefix and postfix forms. *Prefix increment* (++x) increments the value of x *before* its value is used in the expression, while *postfix increment* (x++) increments x *after* its current value is used. The same distinction applies to prefix decrement (--x) and postfix decrement (x--). This subtle difference is crucial. For instance:

```
#include <stdio.h>


int main() {
   int a = 5;
   int b = 5;
   int prefix_increment, postfix_increment;

   prefix_increment = ++a; // a becomes 6, prefix_increment becomes 6
   postfix_increment = b++; // postfix_increment becomes 5, b becomes 6

   printf("Prefix Increment: a = %d, prefix_increment = %d\n", a,
prefix_increment);
   printf("Postfix Increment: b = %d, postfix_increment = %d\n", b,
postfix_increment);

   return 0;
}
```

In this example, ++a increments a to 6 *before* assigning it to prefix_increment, resulting in both a and prefix_increment being 6. Conversely, b++ assigns the current value of b (which is 5) to postfix_increment *then* increments b to 6. Understanding this distinction is vital for avoiding subtle bugs, especially when increment/decrement operators are used within complex expressions or loop conditions (Oualline, 1992). *Operator precedence and associativity* govern the order in which operations are performed in an expression containing multiple operators. Precedence dictates which operator is applied first (e.g., multiplication and division have higher precedence than addition and subtraction). Associativity determines the direction of evaluation for operators with the same precedence (e.g., most arithmetic operators are left-associative, meaning they are evaluated from left to right). For example, in result = 10 + 2 * 3;, multiplication is performed before addition due to higher precedence, yielding result = 16. In result = 10 - 5 - 2;, subtraction is left-associative, evaluated as (10 - 5) - 2, resulting in result = 3. Parentheses () can be used to override precedence and explicitly control the order of evaluation. Using parentheses for clarity, even when not strictly necessary, enhances code readability and reduces ambiguity, particularly in complex expressions. Misunderstanding operator precedence and associativity is a common source of errors, especially for novice programmers. Consulting operator precedence tables and judiciously using parentheses are essential practices for writing correct and predictable C code.

Relational operators compare two operands and determine the relationship between them, resulting in a boolean value (true or false, represented in C as integer 1 or 0 respectively). C provides the relational operators: equal to (==), not equal to (!=), greater than (>), less than (<), greater than or equal to (>=), and less than or equal to (<=). *Logical operators* combine or modify boolean expressions. C provides logical AND (&&), logical OR (||), and logical NOT (!). Logical AND (&&) returns true if both operands are true, otherwise false. Logical OR (||) returns true if at least one operand is true, otherwise false. Logical NOT (!) reverses the logical state of its operand; if the operand is true, ! makes it false, and vice-versa. Relational and logical operators are the foundation of decision-making in programs, used extensively in conditional statements (if, else if, else) and loops (while, for, do-while). Consider a program controlling access to a system based on user credentials: relational operators would be used to compare entered passwords with stored passwords (if (entered_password == stored_password)), and logical operators could combine multiple conditions (e.g., if (username == valid_user && password == correct_password)). *Precedence of relational and logical operators* is also important. Arithmetic operators have higher precedence than relational operators, which in turn have higher precedence than logical operators (except for logical NOT !, which has higher precedence than arithmetic operators). For example, in if (a + b > c && d == e), the addition a + b and comparison d == e are evaluated first, and then the logical AND && is applied to the results of the relational operations. Similar to arithmetic expressions, parentheses can be used to explicitly control the evaluation order in complex boolean expressions and improve readability. A common pitfall is confusing the assignment operator = with the equality operator ==. a = 5; assigns the value 5 to a, while a == 5 checks if a is equal to 5, returning true or false. Using = instead of == in conditional expressions is a frequent source of logic errors that can be difficult to debug.

Bitwise operators operate on individual bits of integer operands. C provides bitwise AND (&), bitwise OR (|), bitwise XOR (^), bitwise NOT (~), left shift (<<), and right shift (>>). Bitwise AND (&) performs a bit-by-bit AND operation. Bitwise OR (|) performs a bit-by-bit OR operation. Bitwise XOR (^) performs a bit-by-bit exclusive OR operation. Bitwise NOT (~) inverts all bits of its operand (unary operator). Left shift (<<) shifts the bits of the left operand to the left by the number of positions specified by the right operand, filling vacated positions with zeros. Right shift (>>) shifts bits to the right. For signed integers, the behavior of right shift (arithmetic vs. logical) can be compiler-dependent; for unsigned integers, it is always a logical right shift (zero-fill). Bitwise operators are often used in low-level programming, embedded systems, and situations where direct manipulation of individual bits is required, such as setting flags, controlling hardware registers, implementing network protocols, and data encryption algorithms. Consider controlling individual LEDs on a microcontroller. Each LED could be associated with a specific bit in a register. Using bitwise OR (|) with a mask (a value with a '1' bit at the desired LED position and '0's elsewhere) can set the corresponding LED on without affecting other LEDs controlled by other bits in the same register. Bitwise AND (&) with a mask and subsequent comparison can check the status of a particular LED. Bitwise XOR (^) can toggle the state of an LED. Understanding bitwise operators unlocks a level of control and efficiency that is essential for certain specialized programming tasks, particularly in systems programming and embedded development (Barr, 2015).

In conclusion, operators are the essential verbs of the C language, enabling programs to perform computations, make decisions, and manipulate data at various levels of abstraction. Mastering assignment, arithmetic, relational, logical, and bitwise operators, understanding their precedence and associativity, and practicing their application in diverse scenarios is crucial for becoming a proficient C programmer. This chapter has laid the groundwork for understanding how operators function as the computational engine of C. The next chapter will build upon this foundation by exploring control flow statements, which use these operators to direct the sequence of program execution based on conditions and iterations.

Chapter 6 Control Flow Statements

In this chapter, you will learn the following:

1. Conditional Statements
    a. if Statement
    b. if-else Structure
    c. if-else-if Ladder
    d. Nested Conditions
    e. Conditional Operator (?:)
    f. switch Statement
2. Looping Structures
    a. for Loop
    b. while Loop
    c. do-while Loop
    d. Nested Loops
3. Jump Statements
    a. break
    b. continue
    c. exit() Function

Control Flow Statements in C

The power of a computer program lies not just in its ability to perform calculations, but also in its capacity to make decisions and repeat actions based on conditions. This dynamic behavior is orchestrated by *control flow statements*, the linguistic tools that dictate the order in which program instructions are executed. Without control flow statements, programs would be limited to linear execution, performing the same sequence of operations every time, regardless of input or conditions. Control flow statements empower programs to become truly intelligent and responsive, adapting their behavior based on data and external events. This chapter will delve into the core control flow mechanisms in C, encompassing conditional statements for decision-making, looping structures for repetitive execution, and jump statements for altering the normal flow of program execution. Mastering these control flow tools is paramount, as they are the key to implementing complex algorithms, creating interactive applications, and building software that can effectively solve real-world problems by responding intelligently to varying circumstances.

Conditional statements enable programs to execute different blocks of code based on whether a specific condition is true or false. The most fundamental conditional statement is the if statement. Its basic structure is if (condition) { /* code to execute if condition is true */ }. The condition is a boolean expression evaluated to either true or false. If true, the code block within the curly braces {} is executed; otherwise, it is skipped. For example, in a temperature monitoring system, an if statement could be used to trigger an alarm if the temperature exceeds a critical threshold: if (temperature > max_temperature) { activate_alarm(); }. Building upon the if statement, the if-else structure provides an alternative code block to execute when the condition is false: if (condition) { /* code if true */ } else { /* code if false */ }. In a login system, an if-else structure can handle both successful and failed login attempts: if (username == valid_user && password == correct_password) { grant_access(); } else { display_error_message(); }. The if-else-if ladder extends conditional logic to handle multiple mutually exclusive conditions. It takes the form: if (condition1) { /* code for condition1 */ } else if (condition2) { /* code for condition2 */ } else if (condition3) { /* ... */ } else { /* default code if none are true */ }. In a program that categorizes student grades, an if-else-if ladder could assign grades based on numerical scores:

```
#include <stdio.h>

int main() {
    int score = 85;
    char grade;

    if (score >= 90) {
        grade = 'A';
    } else if (score >= 80) {
        grade = 'B';
    } else if (score >= 70) {
        grade = 'C';
    } else if (score >= 60) {
        grade = 'D';
    } else {
        grade = 'F';
    }

    printf("Score: %d, Grade: %c\n", score, grade);
    return 0;
}
```

This code snippet demonstrates a step-by-step process of checking score ranges and assigning the corresponding grade. Nested conditions involve placing if statements inside other if or else blocks, allowing for more complex decision-making. For instance, in an e-commerce website, nested conditions could be used to apply discounts based on customer type and purchase amount: if (customer_type == 'premium') { if (purchase_amount > 1000) { apply_discount(0.15); } else { apply_discount(0.10); } } else { apply_discount(0.05); }. The *conditional operator* (?:) provides a concise shorthand for simple if-else structures. It has the syntax: condition ? expression_if_true : expression_if_false. It evaluates condition, and returns expression_if_true if true, and expression_if_false if false. For example, to determine the larger of two numbers concisely: max = (a > b) ? a : b;. This single line effectively achieves the same outcome as a longer if-else block. The switch statement offers an efficient way to handle multi-way branching based on the value of a single variable (often an integer or character). Its structure is: switch (expression) { case value1: /* code for value1 */ break; case value2: /* code for value2 */ break; ... default: /* default code if no case matches */ break; }. The expression is evaluated, and execution jumps to the case label matching the expression's value. The break statement is crucial to exit the switch block after executing a case; without break, execution "falls through" to the next case. A practical application of switch is in command processing:

```
#include <stdio.h>

int main() {
   char command;

   printf("Enter command (a, b, c, or d): ");
   scanf(" %c", &command); // Note the space before %c to consume whitespace

   switch (command) {
      case 'a':
         printf("Executing command A...\n");
         // Code to execute command A
         break;
      case 'b':
         printf("Executing command B...\n");
         // Code to execute command B
```

```
        break;
    case 'c':
        printf("Executing command C...\n");
        // Code to execute command C
        break;
    case 'd':
        printf("Executing command D...\n");
        // Code to execute command D
        break;
    default:
        printf("Invalid command.\n");
        break;
    }

    return 0;
}
```

This example demonstrates processing different commands based on user input using a switch statement. Common pitfalls with conditional statements include incorrect logical expressions, missing break statements in switch cases, and deeply nested if conditions that can become hard to read and maintain. Careful construction of conditions, proper use of break, and refactoring complex nested conditions into more modular functions can mitigate these issues. As McConnell advises in "Code Complete" (McConnell, 2004), strive for clear and concise conditional logic to enhance code readability and reduce the likelihood of errors.

Looping structures enable programs to repeatedly execute a block of code until a certain condition is met. C provides three primary loop types: for, while, and do-while. The for loop is typically used when the number of iterations is known in advance or can be easily determined. Its structure is: for (initialization; condition; increment/decrement) { /* loop body */ }. initialization is executed once at the beginning of the loop. condition is checked before each iteration; if true, the loop body executes; otherwise, the loop terminates. increment/decrement is executed after each iteration, often used to update a loop counter. A common application is iterating through arrays or performing actions a specific number of times. For instance, to calculate the sum of numbers from 1 to 10:

```
#include <stdio.h>

int main() {
   int sum = 0;
   for (int i = 1; i <= 10; i++) {
      sum += i;
   }
   printf("Sum of 1 to 10 is: %d\n", sum);
   return 0;
}
```

This code uses a for loop to iterate from 1 to 10, adding each number to the sum. The while loop repeats a block of code as long as a condition remains true. Its structure is: while (condition) { /* loop body */ }. The condition is checked *before* each iteration. while loops are useful when the number of iterations is not known beforehand, and the loop continues based on an external condition. Reading data from a file until the end of file is reached is a typical while loop application: while ((data = read_from_file()) != EOF) { process_data(data); }. The do-while loop is similar to while, but it checks the condition *after* executing the loop body at least once. Its structure is: do { /* loop body */ } while (condition);. do-while loops are useful when you need to execute the loop body at least once, regardless of the initial condition. Validating user input is a common use case for do-while:

```
#include <stdio.h>

int main() {
   int number;
```

```
  do {
    printf("Enter a positive number: ");
    scanf("%d", &number);
    if (number <= 0) {
      printf("Invalid input. Please enter a positive number.\n");
    }
  } while (number <= 0); // Loop continues as long as input is not positive

  printf("You entered a positive number: %d\n", number);
  return 0;
}
```

This code uses a do-while loop to repeatedly prompt the user for input until a positive number is entered, ensuring at least one input attempt. *Nested loops* involve placing loops inside other loops, useful for processing multi-dimensional data structures or performing iterative operations within iterative processes. Processing a 2D array (matrix) often requires nested loops. Common challenges with loops include infinite loops (where the loop condition never becomes false), off-by-one errors in loop conditions, and inefficient loop design. Careful loop condition construction, proper loop termination logic, and choosing the appropriate loop type for the task are essential for writing correct and efficient looping code. As Kernighan and Ritchie emphasize in "The C Programming Language" (Kernighan & Ritchie, 1988), understanding loop behavior and choosing the right loop structure are fundamental to effective program control.

Jump statements provide mechanisms to alter the normal sequential flow of control within loops and switch statements. The break statement, as seen in switch cases, immediately terminates the innermost enclosing loop (for, while, do-while) or switch statement. It is often used to exit a loop prematurely based on a specific condition, such as finding a desired element in a search algorithm:

```
#include <stdio.h>

int main() {
    int numbers[] = {1, 5, 8, 12, 15, 20};
    int target = 12;
    int found = 0;

    for (int i = 0; i < sizeof(numbers) / sizeof(numbers[0]); i++) {
        if (numbers[i] == target) {
            found = 1;
            printf("Target %d found at index %d.\n", target, i);
            break; // Exit loop once target is found
        }
    }

    if (!found) {
        printf("Target %d not found in the array.\n", target);
    }

    return 0;
}
```

The continue statement skips the rest of the current iteration of a loop and proceeds to the next iteration. It is used to bypass certain processing steps within a loop based on a condition without terminating the entire loop. For instance, to process only odd numbers in a loop: for (int i = 1; i <= 10; i++) { if (i % 2 == 0) { continue; } // Skip even numbers process_odd_number(i); }. The exit() function, declared in <stdlib.h>, terminates the entire program execution immediately. It takes an integer argument, which serves as the program's exit status (0 typically indicates successful termination, non-zero indicates an error). exit() is often used to handle critical errors or exceptional conditions that necessitate program termination: if (memory_allocation_failed()) { fprintf(stderr, "Memory allocation error. Exiting.\n"); exit(1); }. Using exit() should be reserved for exceptional circumstances, as abrupt program termination can sometimes leave resources uncleared or data in an inconsistent state. Using break, continue, and exit() judiciously can enhance program efficiency and error handling, but over-reliance on jump statements can sometimes make code harder to follow and debug, potentially leading to "spaghetti code" if not used carefully (Yourdon & Constantine, 1979).

In summary, control flow statements are the linchpin of dynamic and responsive C programs. Mastering conditional statements for decision-making, looping structures for repetition, and jump statements for flow control manipulation empowers programmers to create sophisticated algorithms and solve complex problems effectively. Understanding the nuances of each control flow statement, practicing their application in diverse scenarios, and adhering to good coding practices for clarity and maintainability are essential steps towards becoming a proficient C programmer. This chapter has provided a comprehensive overview of these fundamental control flow mechanisms. The next chapter will explore functions in C, which are essential for modularizing code and building reusable program components, further extending the programmer's ability to create well-structured and scalable applications.

Chapter 7 Functions in C

In this chapter, you will learn the following:

1. Function Declaration and Definition
2. Returning Values from Functions
3. Standard Library Functions (math.h, string.h, etc.)
4. Passing Arguments to Functions
5. Variable Scope and Lifetime
6. Storage Classes (auto, static, extern, register)
7. Passing by Value vs. Passing by Reference
8. Recursion

Modularizing Code for Reusability and Organization

Functions are the bedrock of structured programming in C, serving as self-contained blocks of code designed to perform specific tasks. Just as a complex machine is assembled from simpler, modular components, well-structured C programs are built from collections of functions, each responsible for a distinct part of the overall functionality. This modular approach promotes code reusability, enhances readability, simplifies debugging, and facilitates collaborative development. Instead of writing monolithic blocks of code, functions allow programmers to break down complex problems into smaller, manageable sub-problems, leading to more organized, efficient, and maintainable software. Understanding functions in C is not just about learning their syntax; it's about adopting a powerful programming paradigm that is essential for building robust and scalable applications. This chapter will comprehensively explore the anatomy of C functions, covering declaration, definition, return values, standard library functions, argument passing mechanisms, variable scope and lifetime, storage classes, parameter passing methods, and the concept of recursion, equipping learners with the skills to effectively leverage functions in their C programming endeavors.

Every function in C must be both *declared* and *defined. Function declaration*, also known as a function prototype, informs the compiler about the function's name, return type, and the types of its parameters (if any) *before* the function is actually used or defined. The declaration typically resides in header files or at the beginning of the source file. The syntax for a function declaration is: return_type function_name(parameter_type1 parameter_name1, parameter_type2 parameter_name2, ...);. For example, int add(int num1, int num2); declares a function named add that takes two integer arguments and returns an integer value. As Kernighan and Ritchie emphasize in "The C Programming Language" (Kernighan & Ritchie, 1988), declarations are crucial for type checking and ensuring that functions are called correctly, preventing type mismatch errors during compilation. *Function definition*, on the other hand, provides the actual implementation of the function – the code block that executes when the function is called. The definition includes the function header (identical to the declaration but without the semicolon at the end) followed by the function body enclosed in curly braces {}. The syntax for a function definition is: return_type function_name(parameter_type1 parameter_name1, parameter_type2 parameter_name2, ...) { /* function body - statements */ }. For example, the definition of the add function declared earlier would be: int add(int num1, int num2) { return num1 + num2; }. The declaration acts as a forward notice to the compiler, while the definition provides the functional code. Separating declaration from definition is particularly important for modular programming and creating reusable libraries, allowing interfaces (declarations) to be separated from implementations (definitions), promoting abstraction and reducing code dependencies (Sommerville, 2011).

Functions can *return values* back to the calling code using the return statement. The return_type in the function declaration and definition specifies the data type of the value returned. If a function is not intended to return any value, its return type is declared as void. The return statement, when executed within a function, immediately terminates the function's execution and returns the specified value (if any) to the caller. For functions with a non-void return type, the return statement must be followed by an expression of a compatible data type. For example, the add function defined earlier returns the integer sum of its two arguments. Consider a function to calculate the area of a circle:

```
#include <stdio.h>

float calculate_circle_area(float radius) {
    const float PI = 3.14159;
    return PI * radius * radius;
}

int main() {
    float radius = 5.0;
    float area = calculate_circle_area(radius);
    printf("Area of circle with radius %.2f is: %.2f\n", radius, area);
    return 0;
}
```

In this example, calculate_circle_area function takes a float radius as input and returns the calculated area as a float. The main() function calls calculate_circle_area, receives the returned area, and prints it. Functions with void return type do not return any value. They are typically used to perform actions or side effects, such as printing output, modifying global variables, or controlling hardware. A function to print a greeting message could be void print_greeting(char name[]) { printf("Hello, %s!\n", name); }. Understanding return values is essential for designing functions that can compute results and pass them back to other parts of the program, enabling modular data processing and computation (Hunt & Thomas, 2000).

C provides a rich set of *standard library functions* that are pre-written and readily available for use in programs. These functions are grouped into libraries, each with a corresponding header file that must be included using the #include preprocessor directive to access the functions. <math.h> provides mathematical functions like sqrt() (square root), pow() (power), sin(), cos(), tan() (trigonometric functions), log() (natural logarithm), and fabs() (absolute value for floating-point numbers). <string.h> offers string manipulation functions such as strlen() (string length), strcpy() (string copy), strcat() (string concatenation), strcmp() (string comparison), and strstr() (substring search). <stdio.h>, as previously discussed, provides input/output functions like printf() and scanf(). Using standard library functions significantly reduces development time and effort by providing well-tested and optimized implementations of common tasks. For instance, calculating the square root of a number can be easily done using sqrt() from <math.h> instead of writing a custom square root algorithm from scratch. Consider a program that calculates the hypotenuse of a right-angled triangle:

```
#include <stdio.h>
#include <math.h>

int main() {
   float side1 = 3.0;
   float side2 = 4.0;
   float hypotenuse = sqrt(pow(side1, 2) + pow(side2, 2));
   printf("Hypotenuse: %.2f\n", hypotenuse);
   return 0;
}
```

This example utilizes pow() and sqrt() functions from <math.h> to efficiently calculate the hypotenuse. Exploring and utilizing standard library functions is a crucial aspect of efficient C programming, leveraging pre-built functionalities to expedite development and improve code robustness (Plauger, 1992).

Functions can receive data as *arguments* or *parameters*. These arguments are passed from the calling code to the function when it is invoked. The function declaration and definition specify the *formal parameters*, including their data types and names. When a function is called, the *actual arguments* provided in the function call are assigned to these formal parameters. C supports *passing arguments by value.* In *pass by value*, a copy of the actual argument's value is passed to the function's formal parameter. Any modifications made to the formal parameter within the function do not affect the original actual argument in the calling code. This mechanism ensures data protection and prevents unintended side effects. For example:

```
#include <stdio.h>

void increment(int num) {
    num++; // Incrementing the formal parameter 'num'
    printf("Inside function: num = %d\n", num);
}

int main() {
    int value = 10;
    printf("Before function call: value = %d\n", value);
    increment(value); // Passing 'value' by value
    printf("After function call: value = %d\n", value);
    return 0;
}
```

In this example, when increment(value) is called, a copy of value (which is 10) is passed to the formal parameter num in the increment function. Inside increment, num is incremented to 11, and this incremented value is printed. However, back in main(), the original value remains unchanged at 10, demonstrating that modifications to the formal parameter in pass by value do not affect the actual argument. Understanding pass by value is crucial for predicting function behavior and ensuring data integrity when passing arguments (Maguire, 1993). (*Pass by reference*, while not directly supported in C in the same way as some other languages, is simulated using pointers, which will be discussed in a later chapter. For now, focus on pass by value.)

Variable scope and lifetime determine where and when variables are accessible and how long they exist in memory. *Scope* refers to the region of the program where a variable can be accessed and used. C has two primary scopes: *local scope* and *global scope.* Variables declared *inside* a function or a block of code (within curly braces {}) have *local scope.* They are accessible only within that function or block and are not visible outside. Local variables are created when the block is entered and destroyed when the block is exited. Variables declared *outside* any function (typically at the top of the source file) have *global scope.* They are accessible from any function within the same source file and potentially across multiple source files in a multi-file program if declared with the extern storage class (discussed later). Global variables exist throughout the program's execution. *Lifetime* refers to the duration for which a variable exists in memory. Local variables typically have *automatic lifetime.* They are automatically created when their scope is entered and automatically destroyed when their scope is exited. Global variables have *static lifetime*; they exist throughout the entire program execution. Understanding scope and lifetime is critical for managing variables effectively, preventing naming conflicts, and controlling memory usage. Using local variables whenever possible promotes modularity and reduces the risk of unintended side effects and naming collisions, contributing to more robust and maintainable code (Anderson, 2006).

Storage classes are keywords in C that specify the scope, lifetime, and linkage of variables and functions. C provides five storage classes: auto, static, extern, and register. auto is the default storage class for local variables. It explicitly declares that a variable has automatic lifetime and local scope. While auto is the default, it is rarely explicitly used in modern C code. static, when applied to a local variable, changes its lifetime from automatic to static. A static local variable retains its value between function calls. It is initialized only once, at the first time the function is called, and its value persists even after the function returns. Its scope remains local to the function in which it is declared. When applied to global variables or functions, static limits their scope to the source file in which they are declared, providing internal linkage (not accessible from other source files). extern is used to declare a global variable or function that is defined in another source file. It provides external linkage, allowing access to variables and functions defined in different compilation units. register is a request to the compiler to store a variable in a CPU register for faster access. However, modern compilers are often sophisticated enough to automatically optimize register allocation, making the register keyword less crucial in many scenarios. The compiler is not obligated to honor the register request, and if it cannot allocate a register, the variable is treated as auto. Understanding storage classes allows for fine-grained control over variable scope, lifetime, and linkage, enabling the creation of modular, efficient, and well-organized C programs, particularly in larger projects involving multiple source files (Banahan, Brady, & Doran, 1991).

Passing by value vs. passing by reference (simulated in C using pointers, introduced later) is a fundamental distinction in how arguments are passed to functions. As previously discussed, C primarily uses *pass by value*. In pass by value, a copy of the actual argument is passed to the formal parameter. Modifications to the formal parameter within the function do not affect the original actual argument. This is the default and most common argument passing mechanism in C. *Passing by reference*, in contrast, would involve passing the *memory address* of the actual argument to the function. In this mechanism, the formal parameter becomes an *alias* for the actual argument, directly accessing and modifying the original data in memory. Languages like C++ directly support pass by reference. In C, pass by reference is *simulated* using pointers. By passing a pointer to a variable as an argument, the function can indirectly access and modify the value at that memory address, effectively achieving pass-by-reference behavior. The detailed mechanism of simulating pass by reference using pointers will be thoroughly explored in the chapter on pointers. For now, it is important to understand that C's default argument passing mechanism is pass by value, and pass by reference-like behavior is achieved using pointers. Choosing between pass by value and pass by reference (or its pointer-based simulation in C) depends on whether the function needs to modify the original argument or just work with a copy of its value. Pass by value protects the original data from unintended modifications, while pass by reference (or pointers) allows functions to directly alter the caller's variables, which is essential in scenarios like swapping variable values or modifying complex data structures in place (Tondo & Gimpel, 1994).

Recursion is a powerful programming technique where a function calls itself, either directly or indirectly. Recursive functions break down a problem into smaller, self-similar subproblems. A recursive function typically has two essential components: a *base case* and a *recursive step*. The *base case* is a condition that, when met, stops the recursion and provides a terminating condition. Without a base case, a recursive function would call itself infinitely, leading to stack overflow and program crash. The *recursive step* is where the function calls itself with a modified input, moving closer to the base case in each recursive call. A classic example of recursion is calculating the factorial of a non-negative integer n (n!). Factorial(0) is defined as 1 (base case). For n > 0, factorial(n) = n * factorial(n-1) (recursive step). Here's a C code example for calculating factorial recursively:

```
#include <stdio.h>

unsigned long long factorial(int n) {
   if (n == 0) { // Base case
      return 1;
   } else { // Recursive step
      return n * factorial(n - 1);
   }
}

int main() {
   int num = 5;
   unsigned long long fact = factorial(num);
   printf("Factorial of %d is: %llu\n", num, fact);
   return 0;
}
```

In this code, factorial(n) function calls itself with n-1 until n becomes 0 (base case), at which point the recursion unwinds, multiplying the intermediate results to compute the final factorial. Recursion is elegant and can provide concise solutions for problems that have a recursive structure, like tree traversals, graph algorithms, and fractals. However, recursive functions can be less efficient than iterative solutions in terms of performance and memory usage due to function call overhead and stack space consumption. Deep recursion without proper base case handling can lead to stack overflow errors, especially for large input values. Therefore, recursion should be used judiciously, considering both its elegance and potential performance implications, and alternative iterative solutions should be considered when efficiency is paramount or stack overflow is a concern (Roberts, 1986).

In conclusion, functions are indispensable tools for structuring, modularizing, and reusing code in C programming. Mastering function declaration, definition, return values, argument passing, scope, lifetime, storage classes, parameter passing methods, and recursion equips programmers with the essential skills to build complex, well-organized, and maintainable C applications. This chapter has laid a comprehensive foundation for understanding and effectively utilizing functions, paving the way for more advanced programming techniques in subsequent chapters.

Chapter 8 Arrays in C

In this chapter, you will learn the following:

1. One-Dimensional Arrays
2. Array Initialization
3. Arrays as Function Arguments
4. Multidimensional Arrays

Structuring Data Collections for Efficient Access

In the landscape of data management within programs, arrays stand as a fundamental and highly versatile data structure. Imagine needing to store a list of student scores, a series of temperature readings from a sensor, or the pixel data for an image. Using individual variables for each data point would quickly become cumbersome and inefficient. Arrays provide an elegant solution by allowing us to group multiple data items of the *same type* under a single name, accessed through an index. This contiguous storage in memory facilitates efficient access and manipulation of data collections, forming the backbone for numerous algorithms and data processing tasks. Understanding arrays in C is not just about learning a syntax for declaring lists; it's about mastering a powerful tool for organizing data logically and accessing it efficiently, a crucial skill for any programmer working with collections of information. This chapter will systematically explore one-dimensional arrays, array initialization techniques, the mechanism of passing arrays to functions, and the concept of multidimensional arrays, equipping learners with the knowledge to effectively utilize arrays for structuring and managing data in their C programs.

One-dimensional arrays, often simply called arrays, are linear sequences of elements of the same data type, stored contiguously in memory. They provide a way to represent ordered lists of items. To declare a one-dimensional array in C, the syntax is: `data_type array_name[array_size];`. For example, `int student_scores[10];` declares an array named `student_scores` that can hold 10 integer values. The `array_size` must be a constant expression known at compile time. Crucially, array indexing in C is zero-based, meaning the first element is accessed using index 0, the second using index 1, and so on, up to index array_size - 1. Accessing elements outside this valid index range (0 to array_size - 1) results in *array index out of bounds*, a common error in C programming that can lead to unpredictable behavior and even program crashes as it might access memory outside the allocated array space. Consider a real-world scenario of managing student grades in a class. An array student_scores could store the grades of each student. To access the grade of the first student, you would use student_scores[0], the second student's grade is student_scores[1], and so forth. Imagine calculating the average score of the class:

```
#include <stdio.h>

int main() {
    int student_scores[5] = {85, 92, 78, 95, 88}; // Example scores
    int sum = 0;
    float average;

    for (int i = 0; i < 5; i++) { // Iterate through the array
        sum += student_scores[i]; // Accumulate sum of scores
    }

    average = (float)sum / 5; // Calculate average

    printf("Average student score: %.2f\n", average);
    return 0;
}
```

This example demonstrates the basic usage of a one-dimensional array to store and process a list of student scores. The for loop iterates through each element of the student_scores array, accessing each score using its index and accumulating the sum. As Hanly and Koffman point out in "Problem Solving and Program Design in C" (Hanly & Koffman, 2009), arrays are particularly well-suited for processing collections of data that have a natural sequential order, facilitating iterative algorithms and data analysis.

Array initialization is the process of assigning initial values to array elements when the array is declared. C offers several ways to initialize arrays. The most common method is to provide an *initializer list* within curly braces {} during array declaration. For example, int numbers[5] = {10, 20, 30, 40, 50}; initializes the numbers array with the specified values. If the initializer list is shorter than the array size, the remaining elements are initialized to zero by default. For example, int values[5] = {1, 2, 3}; will initialize values[0], values[1], and values[2] to 1, 2, and 3 respectively, and values[3] and values[4] will be initialized to 0. If no initializer list is provided, and the array is declared locally (inside a function without static storage class), the array elements will contain *garbage values* (unpredictable values based on whatever was previously in those memory locations). For global or static arrays, elements are initialized to zero by default if no initializer is explicitly provided. Arrays can also be initialized element by element after declaration using a loop:

```
#include <stdio.h>

int main() {
   int data[10];

   for (int i = 0; i < 10; i++) {
      data[i] = i * 2; // Initialize each element with a value
   }

   printf("Initialized array: ");
   for (int i = 0; i < 10; i++) {
      printf("%d ", data[i]); // Print initialized array
   }
   printf("\n");
   return 0;
}
```

This code demonstrates element-wise initialization using a for loop, assigning values based on a formula. Real-world applications of array initialization include setting up initial inventory levels in a stock management system, defining lookup tables with pre-calculated values, or configuring initial states for simulation programs. As King emphasizes in "C Programming: A Modern Approach" (King, 2008), understanding array initialization is crucial for setting up data structures with meaningful starting values, ensuring predictable program behavior from the outset.

Arrays as function arguments are a common and powerful technique in C programming, allowing functions to process collections of data. In C, when an array name is passed as an argument to a function, it *decays to a pointer* to its first element. This means that the function does not receive a copy of the entire array, but rather the memory address of the beginning of the array. Consequently, functions can directly modify the elements of the original array passed as an argument. When declaring a function that takes an array as an argument, you typically specify the parameter as a pointer to the array's element type or use array notation with empty square brackets [] (which is equivalent to a pointer). It is also crucial to pass the *size* of the array as a separate argument, as C functions do not inherently know the size of an array passed as a pointer. Consider a function to calculate the average of an array of numbers:

```
#include <stdio.h>

float calculate_average(int arr[], int size) { // Array as argument, size as argument
   int sum = 0;
   for (int i = 0; i < size; i++) {
      sum += arr[i]; // Accessing array elements within function
   }
   return (float)sum / size;
}
```

```
int main() {
    int scores[] = {75, 80, 90, 85};
    int num_scores = sizeof(scores) / sizeof(scores[0]); // Calculate array size

    float avg_score = calculate_average(scores, num_scores); // Pass array and size
    printf("Average score: %.2f\n", avg_score);
    return 0;
}
```

In this example, calculate_average function takes an integer array arr[] and its size as arguments. It iterates through the array and calculates the average. The main() function passes the scores array and its size to calculate_average. Because arrays are passed as pointers, functions can efficiently process large arrays without the overhead of copying the entire array in memory. However, this also means that if a function modifies array elements passed as arguments, these modifications will be reflected in the original array in the calling code. This is often desirable but should be carefully considered to avoid unintended side effects. As Prata notes in "C Primer Plus" (Prata, 2014), passing arrays to functions as pointers is a key aspect of C's efficiency and flexibility, allowing for powerful data processing capabilities.

Multidimensional arrays extend the concept of arrays to represent data in more than one dimension, most commonly two dimensions (matrices) or three dimensions (e.g., representing 3D space). A two-dimensional array can be visualized as a table of rows and columns. To declare a two-dimensional array, the syntax is: data_type array_name[num_rows][num_columns];. For example, int matrix[3][4]; declares a 2D array named matrix with 3 rows and 4 columns, capable of storing 3 * 4 = 12 integer values. Elements in a 2D array are accessed using two indices: array_name[row_index][column_index], both indices being zero-based.

C stores multidimensional arrays in *row-major order*, meaning elements of the same row are stored contiguously in memory. For example, in matrix[3][4], all elements of row 0 are stored first, followed by elements of row 1, and then row 2. Initialization of multidimensional arrays can be done using nested initializer lists: int matrix[2][3] = {{1, 2, 3}, {4, 5, 6}}; initializes a 2x3 matrix. Real-world applications of multidimensional arrays are abundant. Representing a game board (like chess or tic-tac-toe) can be done using a 2D array. Image processing often utilizes 2D arrays to represent pixel data of images. Spreadsheet applications internally use 2D arrays to manage cells in rows and columns. Consider processing a 2D matrix:

```
#include <stdio.h>

int main() {
   int matrix[2][3] = {{1, 2, 3}, {4, 5, 6}};
   int sum = 0;

   for (int i = 0; i < 2; i++) { // Iterate through rows
      for (int j = 0; j < 3; j++) { // Iterate through columns
         sum += matrix[i][j]; // Access element at row i, column j
         printf("matrix[%d][%d] = %d  ", i, j, matrix[i][j]);
      }
      printf("\n"); // Newline after each row
   }
   printf("Sum of all elements: %d\n", sum);
   return 0;
}
```

This code iterates through a 2D array matrix using nested loops, accessing each element using row and column indices and calculating the sum of all elements. For multidimensional arrays passed as function arguments, the situation is slightly more complex than for one-dimensional arrays. When passing a multidimensional array to a function, you must specify the size of all dimensions *except* the first one (the number of rows is typically not required, but the number of columns and subsequent dimensions *must* be specified in the function parameter declaration). For example, a function taking the matrix above as an argument would be declared as void process_matrix(int mat[][3], int num_rows);. This is because the compiler needs to know the size of the subsequent dimensions to correctly calculate memory addresses for array elements (Schildt, 2000).

In conclusion, arrays are essential data structures in C, providing a powerful and efficient way to manage collections of data. Mastering one-dimensional arrays, array initialization, passing arrays to functions, and multidimensional arrays is crucial for building a wide range of applications in C, from simple data processing tasks to complex simulations and data management systems. Understanding array indexing, initialization methods, and the nuances of passing arrays to functions are key skills for any C programmer. This chapter has laid a solid foundation for working with arrays, and subsequent chapters will build upon these concepts, demonstrating how arrays are used in conjunction with pointers, strings, and more advanced data structures.

Chapter 9 Pointers and Dynamic Memory Allocation

In this chapter, you will learn the following:

1. Introduction to Pointers
2. Pointer Arithmetic
3. Pointers and Arrays
4. Pointers and Functions
5. Dynamic Memory Allocation (malloc(), calloc(), realloc(), free())

Mastering Memory Management in C

Pointers are arguably one of the most powerful and simultaneously most challenging features of the C programming language. Often described as "variables that hold memory addresses," pointers are far more than mere storage containers; they are the key to unlocking direct memory manipulation, enabling dynamic data structures, and achieving highly efficient algorithms. While the concept of pointers might initially seem abstract to novice programmers, a solid understanding of pointers is essential for mastering C and utilizing its full potential, particularly in system programming, embedded systems, and performance-critical applications. This chapter will demystify pointers, starting with a fundamental introduction to their nature and purpose, progressing through pointer arithmetic and their intimate relationship with arrays and functions, and culminating in a comprehensive exploration of dynamic memory allocation using malloc(), calloc(), realloc(), and free(). Embarking on this journey into the realm of pointers is not merely about learning advanced syntax; it's about gaining profound insight into how memory is managed and manipulated at a lower level, empowering you to write truly efficient and flexible C programs.

At its core, a *pointer* in C is a variable whose value is a memory address. Every variable in a program resides at a specific location in memory, identified by a unique address. A pointer variable, instead of directly storing data like an int or float, holds the memory address of another variable. Think of memory addresses as house numbers in a city, and a pointer as a note containing a house number – the pointer itself is not the house, but it tells you where to find the house. To declare a pointer variable, you use the asterisk * along with the data type it points to:

data_type *pointer_name;. For example, int *ptr; declares a pointer variable named ptr that is intended to point to an integer variable. It's crucial to understand that the data type associated with a pointer (e.g., int *) specifies the *type of data* that the pointer *will point to*, not the type of the pointer itself (the pointer itself always holds a memory address, which is essentially an integer). Two key operators are associated with pointers: the *address-of operator* & and the *dereference operator* *. The & operator, when placed before a variable name, yields the memory address of that variable. For instance, ptr = &variable; assigns the memory address of the variable variable to the pointer ptr. The * operator, when placed before a pointer variable, *dereferences* the pointer, meaning it accesses the value stored at the memory address held by the pointer. So, if ptr points to variable, then *ptr is equivalent to variable itself – accessing the value stored at that memory location. Let's illustrate this with a code example:

```
#include <stdio.h>

int main() {
   int num = 10;
   int *ptr; // Declare an integer pointer

   ptr = &num; // ptr now holds the address of num

   printf("Address of num: %p\n", &num); // Print address of num
   printf("Value of ptr: %p\n", ptr);   // Print value of ptr (which is address of num)
   printf("Value of num: %d\n", num);    // Print value of num directly
   printf("Value pointed to by ptr: %d\n", *ptr); // Dereference ptr to get value of
num

   *ptr = 20; // Modify the value at the address pointed to by ptr (which is num)

   printf("Value of num after modification through ptr: %d\n", num); // num is now
20

   return 0;
}
```

In this example, ptr is made to point to num. The code demonstrates how to obtain the address of num using &, assign it to ptr, print the address and the pointer value (which are the same), and then *dereference* ptr using * to access and modify the value of num indirectly through the pointer. As Deitel and Deitel explain in "C: How to Program" (Deitel & Deitel, 2015), pointers provide a level of indirection, allowing you to work with data indirectly through memory addresses, which opens doors to dynamic memory management and advanced data structure implementations.

Pointer arithmetic is a unique feature of C that allows you to perform arithmetic operations on pointer variables. However, pointer arithmetic is not the same as regular integer arithmetic. When you increment or decrement a pointer, or add or subtract an integer from a pointer, the pointer address is *not* simply incremented or decremented by the integer value itself. Instead, the address is adjusted by a multiple of the *size of the data type* that the pointer points to. For example, if ptr is an int * and sizeof(int) is 4 bytes, then ptr++ will increment the address stored in ptr by 4 bytes, effectively making it point to the *next integer* in memory. This scaled arithmetic is crucial for traversing arrays and data structures where elements are stored contiguously. The valid pointer arithmetic operations are: increment (++), decrement (--), addition of an integer to a pointer (ptr + n), subtraction of an integer from a pointer (ptr - n), and subtraction of one pointer from another (pointing to elements of the same array, resulting in the number of elements between them). Operations like pointer addition (ptr1 + ptr2), pointer multiplication, or pointer division are generally *invalid* and not meaningful in C pointer arithmetic. Consider array traversal using pointer arithmetic:

```
#include <stdio.h>

int main() {
  int arr[5] = {100, 200, 300, 400, 500};
  int *ptr = arr; // ptr points to the first element of arr (arr[0])

  printf("Array elements using pointer arithmetic:\n");
  for (int i = 0; i < 5; i++) {
    printf("Element at address %p: %d\n", ptr, *ptr);
    ptr++; // Increment ptr to point to the next integer in arr
  }

  return 0;
}
```

In this example, ptr is initialized to point to the beginning of the arr array. In each iteration of the loop, *ptr accesses the current element, and ptr++ increments the pointer to point to the next element in the array. This demonstrates how pointer arithmetic is naturally scaled to the data type, allowing you to efficiently move from one array element to the next. As Oualline highlights in "Practical C Programming" (Oualline, 1992), pointer arithmetic is a powerful tool for efficient data access and manipulation, especially when working with arrays and memory blocks. However, it is also a source of potential errors if not handled carefully, particularly when dealing with pointer arithmetic across different data types or when going beyond array boundaries.

The relationship between *pointers and arrays* in C is deeply intertwined and fundamental. In C, the name of an array, when used without square brackets [], *decays* to a pointer to its first element. For example, if you have int arr[10];, then arr itself, in most contexts, is treated as a pointer to arr[0]. This means that arr holds the memory address of the first element of the array. Consequently, array indexing arr[i] is fundamentally equivalent to pointer arithmetic and dereferencing *(arr + i). Both expressions access the element at the i-th position relative to the starting address of the array. This equivalence is a cornerstone of C's design and explains why pointer arithmetic is scaled by the data type size – it's designed to work seamlessly with array element access. This duality allows you to use pointer notation to access array elements and vice-versa. For instance, to access the third element of arr (which is at index 2), you can use either arr[2] or *(arr + 2). This interchangeability is a powerful feature, allowing for flexible and often more efficient array manipulation using pointers. Consider a function to sum array elements using pointer notation:

```
#include <stdio.h>

int sum_array(int *arr_ptr, int size) { // Array parameter as pointer
   int sum = 0;
   for (int i = 0; i < size; i++) {
      sum += *(arr_ptr + i); // Access array elements using pointer arithmetic
   }
   return sum;
}

int main() {
   int numbers[] = {1, 2, 3, 4, 5};
   int array_size = sizeof(numbers) / sizeof(numbers[0]);
   int total_sum = sum_array(numbers, array_size); // Pass array name (pointer)

   printf("Sum of array elements: %d\n", total_sum);

   return 0;
}
```

In this example, sum_array takes an int *arr_ptr as a parameter, treating the array as a pointer to its first element. Inside the function, pointer arithmetic *(arr_ptr + i) is used to access array elements. The main() function passes the array name numbers directly to sum_array, which is automatically treated as a pointer to the beginning of the array. As Schildt emphasizes in "C: The Complete Reference" (Schildt, 2000), the pointer-array relationship is a fundamental aspect of C, providing both flexibility and efficiency in array handling. However, it's crucial to remember that array names decay to pointers only in certain contexts (like function arguments). In other contexts, like sizeof(arr), arr refers to the entire array and not just a pointer to the first element.

Pointers and functions interact in several important ways. As seen in the previous section, functions can accept pointers as arguments, enabling them to work with arrays efficiently. Furthermore, passing pointers to functions is the mechanism in C for simulating *pass-by-reference.* By passing a pointer to a variable as an argument, a function can indirectly modify the original variable in the calling function. This is because the function receives the memory address of the variable, and dereferencing the pointer within the function allows it to access and modify the data at that address, which is the original variable itself. Let's illustrate pass-by-reference simulation using pointers with a swap function:

```
#include <stdio.h>

void swap(int *a, int *b) { // Function taking pointers as arguments
   int temp = *a; // temp stores the value pointed to by a
   *a = *b;       // Value at address pointed to by a is replaced with value at address
pointed to by b
   *b = temp;     // Value at address pointed to by b is replaced with value in temp
}

int main() {
   int x = 10, y = 20;

   printf("Before swap: x = %d, y = %d\n", x, y);
   swap(&x, &y); // Passing addresses of x and y to swap function
   printf("After swap: x = %d, y = %d\n", x, y);

   return 0;
}
```

In this example, the swap function takes two *integer pointers* *a and *b as arguments. Inside swap, pointer dereferencing is used to access and modify the values at the memory locations pointed to by a and b. In main(), the addresses of x and y are passed to swap using the & operator. After calling swap, the values of x and y are indeed swapped, demonstrating the effect of pass-by-reference simulation using pointers. Functions can also *return pointers*. A function can return the address of a variable, particularly dynamically allocated memory. However, returning pointers requires careful memory management. It's crucial to ensure that the memory pointed to by the returned pointer remains valid after the function returns and is properly deallocated to prevent memory leaks. Returning pointers to local variables declared within a function is generally *dangerous* because local variables are destroyed when the function exits, leading to dangling pointers that point to invalid memory. Returning pointers to dynamically allocated memory or global/static variables is safer, provided that memory deallocation is handled correctly later.

Dynamic memory allocation is a crucial technique in C that allows programs to allocate memory *at runtime* as needed, rather than having to pre-allocate a fixed amount of memory at compile time. C provides several standard library functions for dynamic memory allocation, all declared in <stdlib.h>. malloc(size) allocates a block of memory of the specified size (in bytes) and returns a void * pointer to the beginning of the allocated block. void * is a generic pointer type that can be cast to any other pointer type. calloc(num_elements, element_size) allocates memory for an array of num_elements, where each element is of size element_size bytes. calloc() also initializes all allocated bytes to zero, unlike malloc(), which does not initialize memory. realloc(ptr, new_size) resizes a previously allocated memory block pointed to by ptr to new_size. It may move the memory block if necessary and returns a pointer to the resized block. free(ptr) deallocates a memory block previously allocated by malloc(), calloc(), or realloc() and pointed to by ptr. It is essential to free() dynamically allocated memory when it is no longer needed to prevent *memory leaks*, where allocated memory is not released back to the system, leading to resource exhaustion over time. Let's illustrate dynamic memory allocation to create an array of variable size:

```
#include <stdio.h>
#include <stdlib.h> // For malloc, calloc, realloc, free

int main() {
    int n;
    int *dynamic_array;

    printf("Enter the size of the array: ");
    scanf("%d", &n);

    dynamic_array = (int *)malloc(n * sizeof(int)); // Allocate memory for n integers

    if (dynamic_array == NULL) { // Check if malloc was successful
        fprintf(stderr, "Memory allocation failed!\n");
        return 1; // Indicate error
    }

    printf("Enter %d elements for the array:\n", n);
    for (int i = 0; i < n; i++) {
        scanf("%d", &dynamic_array[i]); // Access dynamically allocated array like a
regular array
    }

    printf("You entered array elements: ");
    for (int i = 0; i < n; i++) {
        printf("%d ", dynamic_array[i]);
    }
    printf("\n");

    free(dynamic_array); // Deallocate dynamically allocated memory

    return 0;
```

```
}
```

This example demonstrates dynamic memory allocation using malloc() to create an integer array of size n determined at runtime. It includes error checking to handle potential memory allocation failure (if malloc() returns NULL). The dynamically allocated array is used like a regular array, and importantly, free(dynamic_array) is called at the end to release the allocated memory. Dynamic memory allocation is crucial for creating data structures of variable size, handling input data of unknown size, and implementing complex data structures like linked lists and trees, where memory requirements may change during program execution. As Kernighan and Ritchie emphasize in "The C Programming Language" (Kernighan & Ritchie, 1988), dynamic memory allocation provides the flexibility needed to build powerful and adaptable programs that can handle varying data sizes and complex memory management scenarios. However, it also introduces the responsibility of careful memory management, with potential pitfalls like memory leaks and dangling pointers if free() is not used correctly or if memory is freed prematurely or multiple times.

In conclusion, pointers and dynamic memory allocation are powerful and essential features of C, providing fine-grained control over memory and enabling the implementation of sophisticated data structures and algorithms. Mastering pointer concepts, pointer arithmetic, their relationship with arrays and functions, and the techniques of dynamic memory allocation and deallocation is crucial for any serious C programmer. This chapter has provided a comprehensive introduction to these topics, laying the groundwork for understanding more advanced C programming techniques that heavily rely on pointers and dynamic memory management. The next chapters will build upon these foundations, exploring how pointers and dynamic memory allocation are used in strings, structures, file handling, and advanced data structures.

Chapter 10 Strings in C

In this chapter, you will learn the following:

1. Character Arrays and Strings
2. String Manipulation Functions (strlen(), strcpy(), strcmp(), etc.)
3. String Handling in Functions

Weaving Textual Data into Programs

Strings, the fundamental units for representing textual information, are ubiquitous in computing. From user interfaces and text editors to network communication protocols and data parsing, strings are the primary means by which programs interact with and process human-readable text. While some programming languages treat strings as a distinct built-in data type, C takes a more foundational approach, representing strings as *character arrays* terminated by a null character (\0). This representation, deeply rooted in C's memory-centric nature, provides programmers with fine-grained control over string manipulation but also demands a thorough understanding of their underlying structure and potential pitfalls. Mastering strings in C is not merely about manipulating text; it's about appreciating C's low-level approach to data representation and leveraging character arrays effectively to handle textual data, a skill essential for diverse applications ranging from system utilities to data processing tools. This chapter will comprehensively explore character arrays as strings, delve into standard string manipulation functions provided by the C library, and examine best practices for handling strings within functions, equipping learners with the knowledge to confidently work with textual data in their C programs.

At its heart, a *string in C* is simply an array of characters, where the end of the string is explicitly marked by a null character, represented as \0. This null character is a character with ASCII value 0 and is crucial; it signals to string-handling functions where the string ends. Without it, functions would not know where the string terminates in memory and could potentially read beyond the intended boundaries, leading to errors.

To declare a character array intended to hold a string, you use the char data type and specify the array size large enough to accommodate the string and the null terminator: char string_variable[size];. For instance, char message[50]; declares a character array named message capable of holding a string of up to 49 characters (plus the null terminator). Strings can be initialized during declaration in several ways. One common method is using a *string literal*, which is a sequence of characters enclosed in double quotes: char greeting[] = "Hello";. In this case, the compiler automatically allocates an array large enough to hold "Hello" and the null terminator and initializes it accordingly. Note that greeting is declared without an explicit size; the compiler infers the size from the string literal. Another way is to initialize element by element: char name[5] = {'J', 'o', 'h', 'n', '\0'};. Here, we explicitly include the null terminator. If you initialize a character array with a string literal that exactly fills the array, the compiler will *not* automatically add a null terminator, which can lead to problems when using standard string functions. It's crucial to ensure that character arrays intended for strings are always null-terminated to be correctly processed by string functions. As Kernighan and Ritchie demonstrate in "The C Programming Language" (Kernighan & Ritchie, 1988), the null-terminated convention is a fundamental aspect of C strings, and understanding its importance is paramount for working with textual data in C.

C's standard library, specifically <string.h>, provides a rich set of *string manipulation functions* that greatly simplify common string operations. strlen(str) is a fundamental function that calculates the *length* of a string, returning the number of characters *before* the null terminator. It does *not* count the null terminator itself. For example, strlen("Hello") would return

5. strcpy(destination, source) is used to *copy* a string source to another string destination. It copies the entire string from source, including the null terminator, to destination. It's crucial to ensure that the destination array is large enough to hold the entire source string to prevent *buffer overflow*, a serious security vulnerability where data is written beyond the allocated buffer, potentially overwriting adjacent memory and causing crashes or security breaches. Safer alternatives like strncpy(destination, source, n) are available, which copy at most n characters from source to destination. However, strncpy might not always null-terminate the destination string if source is longer than or equal to n, requiring manual null termination in such cases. strcmp(str1, str2) is used to *compare* two strings lexicographically (dictionary order). It returns 0 if str1 and str2 are equal, a negative value if str1 comes before str2 lexicographically, and a positive value if str1 comes after str2. This function is essential for sorting strings, searching in dictionaries, and making decisions based on string comparisons. Let's illustrate the usage of these functions:

```
#include <stdio.h>
#include <string.h>

int main() {
    char message1[20] = "Hello";
    char message2[20];
    int length;
    int comparison;

    length = strlen(message1);
    printf("Length of message1: %d\n", length); // Output: Length of message1: 5

    strcpy(message2, message1);
    printf("message2 after strcpy: %s\n", message2); // Output: message2 after strcpy:
Hello

    comparison = strcmp(message1, message2);
    if (comparison == 0) {
```

```
        printf("message1 and message2 are equal.\n"); // Output: message1 and
message2 are equal.
    } else {
        printf("message1 and message2 are not equal.\n");
    }

    comparison = strcmp(message1, "World");
    if (comparison < 0) {
        printf("message1 comes before 'World' lexicographically.\n"); // Output:
message1 comes before 'World' lexicographically.
    } else if (comparison > 0) {
        printf("message1 comes after 'World' lexicographically.\n");
    }

    return 0;
}
```

This example demonstrates basic usage of strlen, strcpy, and strcmp. Other important string functions in <string.h> include strcat(destination, source) for concatenating (appending) source to the end of destination (again, buffer overflow risk exists, safer strncat is recommended), strchr(str, char) to find the first occurrence of a character in a string, and strstr(haystack, needle) to search for the first occurrence of a substring needle within a string haystack. As Schildt notes in "C: The Complete Reference" (Schildt, 2000), these standard library functions provide efficient and readily available tools for performing common string operations, significantly simplifying text processing in C programs. However, it's crucial to be aware of potential buffer overflow issues with functions like strcpy and strcat and utilize safer alternatives or implement bounds checking when necessary, especially when dealing with user input or external data sources.

String handling in functions in C is particularly important, as functions are the building blocks of modular and reusable code. When passing strings to functions in C, remember that character arrays, like other arrays, *decay to pointers* to their first element. Therefore, when you pass a character array (string) to a function, you are actually passing a char * pointer to the first character of the string. This implies that functions can directly modify the string passed as an argument, as they are working with the original memory location. When declaring a function that accepts a string argument, you typically declare the parameter as char * or char [] (which are equivalent in function parameter declarations). It is also common practice to pass the length of the string as a separate argument if the function needs to know the string's length and cannot rely on strlen within the function (e.g., for efficiency reasons or if dealing with potentially non-null-terminated character arrays in specific scenarios, though null-termination is the standard convention for C strings). Consider a function to convert a string to uppercase:

```
#include <stdio.h>
#include <string.h>
#include <ctype.h> // For toupper()

void string_to_uppercase(char str[]) { // String argument as char array (pointer)
   for (int i = 0; str[i] != '\0'; i++) { // Iterate until null terminator
      str[i] = toupper(str[i]); // Convert each character to uppercase
   }
}

int main() {
   char text[] = "hello world";
   printf("Original string: %s\n", text); // Output: Original string: hello world
   string_to_uppercase(text); // Pass string to function (as pointer)
   printf("Uppercase string: %s\n", text); // Output: Uppercase string: HELLO
WORLD
   return 0;
}
```

In this example, string_to_uppercase function takes a char str[] (which is treated as char *str) as input. It iterates through the string until the null terminator is encountered and converts each character to uppercase using toupper() from <ctype.h>. In main(), the text array is passed to string_to_uppercase, and after the function call, the original text array in main() is modified to uppercase, demonstrating that functions can directly alter strings passed as arguments. As Prata emphasizes in "C Primer Plus" (Prata, 2014), understanding that strings are passed as pointers to functions is crucial for predicting function behavior and effectively manipulating textual data within modular C programs. When designing functions that handle strings, it's important to be mindful of buffer sizes, potential null termination issues, and whether the function should modify the original string or work with a copy.

A common challenge when working with strings in C is *buffer overflow*. Functions like strcpy and strcat, if used carelessly, can write beyond the bounds of the destination buffer, leading to security vulnerabilities and program instability. Always ensure that the destination buffer is large enough to accommodate the copied or concatenated string, or use safer alternatives like strncpy and strncat with explicit size limits, remembering to handle potential null termination issues with these safer functions. Another common pitfall is *off-by-one errors* when manually manipulating strings or iterating through character arrays. Carefully check loop conditions and index boundaries to avoid accessing memory outside the allocated array range. Always remember the null terminator's role and ensure that strings are properly null-terminated, especially after manual string manipulations or when creating strings dynamically. Using debugging tools and memory checkers (like Valgrind) can be invaluable in detecting buffer overflows and memory-related errors when working with strings in C. Adopting defensive programming practices, such as input validation and careful buffer management, is essential for writing robust and secure C programs that handle strings reliably.

In summary, strings in C, represented as null-terminated character arrays, are a fundamental data type for handling textual information. Mastering character array declaration, initialization, standard string manipulation functions from <string.h>, and understanding string handling in functions are essential skills for any C programmer. Being mindful of buffer overflows, null termination, and adopting safe string handling practices are crucial for writing robust and secure C programs that effectively process textual data. This chapter has provided a comprehensive introduction to strings in C, building upon the foundational concepts of arrays and pointers. The next chapter will delve into structures and unions, which allow for grouping data of different types together into custom data structures, further expanding the capabilities of C for organizing and managing complex data in programs.

© 2025 Mark John Lado

Chapter 11 Structures and Unions

In this chapter, you will learn the following:

1. Defining and Using Structures
2. Nested Structures
3. Array of Structures
4. Pointers to Structures
5. Unions in C

Crafting Custom Data Types in C

As programs grow in complexity, the need to manage intricate and heterogeneous data becomes paramount. While arrays efficiently handle collections of homogeneous data, real-world applications often involve data entities composed of elements of different types. Consider representing a student record, which might include a name (string), an ID (integer), and GPA (float). Using separate arrays for each attribute would be cumbersome and difficult to manage as a single logical unit. Structures in C provide a powerful solution to this challenge by enabling the creation of *user-defined data types* that can group together variables of different data types under a single name. Unions, a related concept, offer a memory-efficient way to store different data types within the same memory location, though with different usage paradigms. Mastering structures and unions is not merely about expanding your C syntax repertoire; it's about acquiring the ability to model complex real-world entities directly within your programs, leading to more organized, readable, and maintainable code, especially crucial in larger software projects and data-intensive applications. This chapter will comprehensively explore the definition, usage, and advanced features of structures, along with an introduction to unions and their specific applications, equipping learners with the tools to design and implement custom data types tailored to their programming needs.

Structures in C are composite data types that allow you to group together variables of different data types under a single name. They are also known as *user-defined data types* or *aggregate data types*. To define a structure, you use the `struct` keyword followed by a structure tag (name) and a list of *members* enclosed in curly braces {}. The syntax for structure definition is: struct structure_tag { data_type member1; data_type member2; ... };. For example, to define a structure to represent a point in 2D space: struct Point { int x; int y; };. This definition creates a new data type named struct Point. Notice that the structure definition itself does not create any variables; it merely defines the blueprint for creating structure variables. To declare a variable of a structure type, you use the struct keyword followed by the structure tag and the variable name: struct Point p1;. This declaration creates a variable p1 of type struct Point, which can hold two integer members, x and y. To access individual members of a structure variable, you use the *dot operator* (.). For example, to set the x and y coordinates of p1: p1.x = 10; p1.y = 20;. To access and print the coordinates: printf("Point p1: (%d, %d)\n", p1.x, p1.y);. Structures can be initialized during declaration as well, similar to arrays, using an initializer list within curly braces: struct Point p2 = {30, 40};. Consider a real-world application of representing employee records in a human resource management system. A structure Employee could group together employee name, ID, salary, and department:

```
#include <stdio.h>
#include <string.h> // For strcpy

struct Employee {
   char name[50];
   int employee_id;
   float salary;
   char department[30];
};

int main() {
   struct Employee emp1; // Declare a structure variable

   // Initialize members
   strcpy(emp1.name, "John Doe");
   emp1.employee_id = 12345;
```

```
    emp1.salary = 60000.00;
    strcpy(emp1.department, "Engineering");

    // Print employee information
    printf("Employee Name: %s\n", emp1.name);
    printf("Employee ID: %d\n", emp1.employee_id);
    printf("Salary: %.2f\n", emp1.salary);
    printf("Department: %s\n", emp1.department);

    return 0;
}
```

This example illustrates defining a structure Employee and using it to create and initialize an employee record. Structures provide a logical way to group related data, enhancing code organization and readability. As Deitel and Deitel emphasize in "C: How [1] to Program" (Deitel & Deitel, 2015), structures are essential for creating custom data types that mirror real-world entities, making code more intuitive and easier to manage.

Nested structures allow you to define structures within other structures, creating hierarchical data organizations. This is particularly useful for representing complex entities with sub-components or relationships. For example, to represent a rectangle, you could use a structure Rectangle that contains two Point structures representing the top-left and bottom-right corners.

```
#include <stdio.h>

struct Point {
    int x;
    int y;
};

struct Rectangle {
    struct Point topLeft; // Nested Point structure
    struct Point bottomRight; // Nested Point structure
};
```

```
int main() {
    struct Rectangle rect1;

    // Initialize rectangle corners
    rect1.topLeft.x = 10;
    rect1.topLeft.y = 20;
    rect1.bottomRight.x = 50;
    rect1.bottomRight.y = 10;

    // Calculate and print rectangle area (example calculation - simplified for
illustration)
    int width = rect1.bottomRight.x - rect1.topLeft.x;
    int height = rect1.topLeft.y - rect1.bottomRight.y; // Assuming top-left y >
bottom-right y
    int area = width * height;

    printf("Rectangle Area: %d\n", area); // Output: Rectangle Area: 1600

    return 0;
}
```

In this example, Rectangle structure nests two Point structures, topLeft and bottomRight. To access members of the nested structures, you use multiple dot operators chained together, like rect1.topLeft.x. Nested structures allow for representing complex relationships and hierarchies within data. Consider a system for managing addresses. An Address structure might be nested within a Person structure, representing a person's contact information more comprehensively. As Prata illustrates in "C Primer Plus" (Prata, 2014), nested structures are a powerful tool for modeling complex data relationships and creating more organized and modular data representations.

An *array of structures* is created when you need to store a collection of structure variables of the same type. This is particularly useful when you have a list of entities, each represented by a structure. For example, to store information for multiple employees, you can create an array of Employee structures.

```
#include <stdio.h>
#include <string.h>

struct Employee {
    char name[50];
    int employee_id;
    float salary;
    char department[30];
};

int main() {
    struct Employee employees[3]; // Array of 3 Employee structures

    // Initialize the first employee
    strcpy(employees[0].name, "Alice Smith");
    employees[0].employee_id = 20001;
    employees[0].salary = 75000.00;
    strcpy(employees[0].department, "Marketing");

    // Initialize the second employee
    strcpy(employees[1].name, "Bob Johnson");
    employees[1].employee_id = 20002;
    employees[1].salary = 80000.00;
    strcpy(employees[1].department, "Sales");

    // Initialize the third employee
    strcpy(employees[2].name, "Charlie Brown");
    employees[2].employee_id = 20003;
    employees[2].salary = 70000.00;
    strcpy(employees[2].department, "HR");

    // Print information for all employees
    for (int i = 0; i < 3; i++) {
        printf("\nEmployee %d:\n", i + 1);
        printf("Name: %s\n", employees[i].name);
        printf("ID: %d\n", employees[i].employee_id);
        printf("Salary: %.2f\n", employees[i].salary);
        printf("Department: %s\n", employees[i].department);
    }

    return 0;
}
```

This code creates an array employees of three Employee structures. Each element of the array employees[0], employees[1], employees[2] is a structure variable of type struct Employee. You access members of individual structures in the array using array indexing and the dot operator, like employees[i].name. Arrays of structures are fundamental for managing lists of structured data, such as databases of records, inventories of items, or collections of objects in simulations. As Schildt points out in "C: The Complete Reference" (Schildt, 2000), arrays of structures combine the organizational power of structures with the efficient data access of arrays, making them highly versatile for data management in C.

Pointers to structures are pointers that hold the memory address of a structure variable. They are essential for dynamic memory allocation of structures and for implementing pass-by-reference semantics for structures in functions. To declare a pointer to a structure, you use the struct keyword, the structure tag, and the asterisk *: struct structure_tag *pointer_name;. For example, struct Point *ptr_p; declares a pointer ptr_p that can point to a struct Point variable. You can assign the address of a structure variable to a structure pointer using the address-of operator &: struct Point p3; ptr_p = &p3;. To access members of a structure through a pointer, you can use the dereference operator * and the dot operator, like (*ptr_p).x. However, C provides a more convenient operator for this purpose: the *arrow operator* (->). The expression ptr_p->x is equivalent to (*ptr_p).x, both accessing the x member of the structure pointed to by ptr_p. Dynamic memory allocation for structures is commonly done using malloc() or calloc() and structure pointers. For example, to dynamically allocate memory for a struct Point: struct Point *dynamic_point = (struct Point *)malloc(sizeof(struct Point));. After allocation, you can access and modify members using the arrow operator: dynamic_point->x = 100; dynamic_point->y = 200;. Remember to free() dynamically allocated structure memory when it's no longer needed to prevent memory leaks: free(dynamic_point);. Let's illustrate pointers to structures with a function that modifies a point structure through a pointer:

```
#include <stdio.h>
#include <stdlib.h> // For malloc, free

struct Point {
   int x;
   int y;
};

void move_point(struct Point *p, int delta_x, int delta_y) { // Function takes
structure pointer
   p->x += delta_x; // Modify x member through pointer
   p->y += delta_y; // Modify y member through pointer
}

int main() {
   struct Point *point_ptr = (struct Point *)malloc(sizeof(struct Point));
   if (point_ptr == NULL) {
      fprintf(stderr, "Memory allocation failed!\n");
      return 1;
   }

   point_ptr->x = 5;
   point_ptr->y = 8;

   printf("Point before move: (%d, %d)\n", point_ptr->x, point_ptr->y); // Output:
Point before move: (5, 8)
   move_point(point_ptr, 10, -2); // Pass structure pointer to function
   printf("Point after move: (%d, %d)\n", point_ptr->x, point_ptr->y);  // Output:
Point after move: (15, 6)

   free(point_ptr); // Deallocate dynamic memory

   return 0;
}
```

In this example, move_point function takes a struct Point *p as input, allowing it to modify the x and y members of the Point structure pointed to by p. Pointers to structures are essential for dynamic data structures like linked lists and trees, where structures are linked together using pointers, and dynamic memory allocation is used to create and manage nodes in these structures. They are also crucial for implementing efficient algorithms that operate on structured data, as passing pointers to structures avoids the overhead of copying entire structure variables, especially when dealing with large structures.

Unions in C are another type of user-defined data type, similar to structures but with a key difference: all members of a union *share the same memory location*. This means that only one member of a union can be active (hold a valid value) at any given time. The size of a union is determined by the size of its largest member. To define a union, you use the union keyword followed by a union tag and a list of members: union union_tag { data_type member1; data_type member2; ... };. For example, to define a union that can hold either an integer or a float: union Data { int i; float f; };. To declare a union variable: union Data data_var;. You access members of a union using the dot operator (.) just like structures. However, assigning a value to one member of a union overwrites the value of any other member that previously occupied the same memory location. Unions are primarily used for *memory saving* when you need to store different types of data in the same memory location at *different times* but not simultaneously. They are useful in situations where memory is constrained, or when you need to interpret the same memory location in different ways depending on the context. Consider a scenario where you need to represent a value that can be either an integer ID or a string name, but not both at the same time:

```
#include <stdio.h>
#include <string.h>

union Value {
    int id;
    char name[30];
};

int main() {
    union Value val;

    val.id = 123;
    printf("Value as ID: %d\n", val.id); // Output: Value as ID: 123
    // At this point, val.id is valid, but val.name's content is undefined

    strcpy(val.name, "John Doe"); // Overwrite union memory with name
    printf("Value as Name: %s\n", val.name); // Output: Value as Name: John Doe
    // Now, val.name is valid, but val.id's value is no longer reliable

    // Accessing val.id after setting val.name can lead to unexpected results as the
memory has been overwritten.
    printf("Value as ID (after setting name - unreliable): %d\n", val.id); // Output:
Value as ID (after setting name - unreliable): some garbage value

    return 0;
}
```

In this example, val is a union. First, val.id is assigned a value, and then val.name is assigned a string. Note that after assigning to val.name, the value of val.id becomes unreliable because both members share the same memory. Unions are often used in conjunction with structures to create *tagged unions* or *variant records*, where a structure contains a union and a tag member that indicates which member of the union is currently active and should be interpreted. This approach allows you to create flexible data structures that can hold different types of data based on a tag value. However, using unions requires careful programming to ensure that you are always accessing the currently active member and interpreting the data correctly, as misuse can lead to data corruption and unexpected program behavior (Harbison & Steele, 2002).

In conclusion, structures and unions are powerful tools in C for creating custom data types and managing complex data. Structures enable grouping heterogeneous data into logical units, enhancing code organization and readability. Nested structures and arrays of structures further extend their capabilities for modeling complex data relationships and collections. Pointers to structures facilitate dynamic memory allocation and efficient data manipulation. Unions offer a memory-saving approach for storing different data types in the same memory location, useful in specific scenarios where memory optimization is crucial. Mastering structures and unions is essential for developing robust, efficient, and well-organized C programs that can effectively handle complex data requirements in a wide range of applications. This chapter has provided a comprehensive introduction to these concepts, laying the foundation for their application in more advanced C programming techniques and data structure implementations.

Chapter 12 File Handling in C

In this chapter, you will learn the following:

1. Introduction to File Handling
2. Opening and Closing Files
3. Reading and Writing Files
4. File Pointers and Modes
5. Error Handling in File Operations

Bridging the Gap Between Programs and Persistent Data

In the dynamic world of computing, programs often need to interact with data that persists beyond their execution lifecycle. This necessity arises from diverse needs, ranging from storing user preferences and application settings to processing large datasets and managing system logs. *File handling* in C provides the mechanism for programs to interact with external files stored on a storage medium (like a hard drive or SSD), allowing them to read data from files and write data to files, effectively bridging the gap between transient program execution and persistent data storage. Imagine a word processor needing to save documents, a database system managing records, or a web server serving web pages from files; all these functionalities rely fundamentally on file handling capabilities. Understanding file handling in C is not merely about learning file I/O functions; it's about grasping how programs interact with the operating system to access and manage files, a crucial skill for building applications that can persist data, process external inputs, and generate outputs that can be used beyond the immediate program run. This chapter will embark on a comprehensive exploration of file handling in C, covering file operations from opening and closing files to reading, writing, and robust error handling, equipping learners with the knowledge to seamlessly integrate persistent data management into their C programs.

The first step in interacting with a file in C is to *open* it. Opening a file establishes a connection between your program and the physical file on the storage device. In C, the fopen() function, declared in <stdio.h>, is used to open a file. The fopen() function takes two crucial arguments: the *filename* (a string representing the path to the file) and the *mode* (a string specifying the intended operation on the file – read, write, append, etc.). The function returns a *file pointer* of type FILE *, which acts as a handle to the opened file. If fopen() fails to open the file (e.g., file not found, permission denied), it returns NULL. It's *critical* to check the return value of fopen() to ensure that the file was opened successfully before attempting any file operations. As Deitel and Deitel emphasize in "C: How to Program" (Deitel & Deitel, 2015), robust error checking is paramount in file handling to prevent unexpected program behavior and potential crashes. Once you have finished working with a file, it is essential to *close* it using the fclose() function, also declared in <stdio.h>. fclose() takes the file pointer (returned by fopen()) as its argument and breaks the connection between the program and the file, ensuring that any buffered data is flushed to the file and system resources are released. Failing to close files can lead to data loss, resource leaks, and potential file corruption. Here's a simple example demonstrating opening and closing a file:

```
#include <stdio.h>

int main() {
    FILE *fptr; // Declare a file pointer

    // Open a file in write mode ("w")
    fptr = fopen("myfile.txt", "w");

    if (fptr == NULL) {
        printf("Error opening file!\n"); // Error checking
        return 1; // Indicate error
    }

    printf("File 'myfile.txt' opened successfully for writing.\n");

    fclose(fptr); // Close the file
```

```
    printf("File 'myfile.txt' closed.\n");

    return 0;
}
```

This code snippet demonstrates opening a file named "myfile.txt" in write mode using fopen(). It checks if fopen() returned NULL indicating an error. If successful, it prints a success message and then closes the file using fclose(). The file modes in fopen() are crucial. Common modes include: "r" (read mode), "w" (write mode - creates a new file or overwrites an existing one), "a" (append mode - creates a new file or appends to an existing one), "r+" (read and write mode, starting from the beginning of the file), "w+" (read and write mode, truncates or creates a new file), and "a+" (read and append mode, creates a new file or appends to an existing one, read access from the beginning of the file). Binary file modes, like "rb", "wb", "ab", "r+b", "w+b", and "a+b", are used for binary files (non-textual data), treating file content as raw bytes without text-specific interpretations. Choosing the appropriate file mode is crucial and depends on the intended operation: read if you only need to read data, write if you want to create a new file or overwrite an existing one, and append if you want to add data to the end of an existing file without overwriting its content.

Once a file is opened, you can perform *reading* and *writing* operations. C provides a variety of functions for reading and writing data to files, catering to different data formats and input/output needs. For *formatted output* to a file, fprintf() function is used, analogous to printf() but taking an additional first argument – the file pointer to write to. fprintf(fptr, "Formatted text: %d, %.2f\n", integer_value, float_value); writes formatted output to the file pointed to by fptr. For *formatted input* from a file, fscanf()

is used, similarly analogous to scanf() but reading from a file pointer. fscanf(fptr, "%d %f", &integer_variable, &float_variable); reads formatted input from the file pointed to by fptr and stores it in the specified variables. For *character-based input/output*, fputc(character, fptr) writes a single character to a file, and fgetc(fptr) reads a single character from a file, returning the character or EOF (End Of File) if the end of the file is reached or an error occurs. For *line-based input/output* (reading and writing entire lines of text), fgets(buffer, size, fptr) reads at most size - 1 characters from a file into a character array buffer, stopping at a newline character or EOF and null-terminating the string in buffer. fputs(string, fptr) writes a string to a file. For *block-based input/output* (reading and writing blocks of raw bytes, useful for binary files), fread(buffer, size, count, fptr) reads up to count items of size bytes each from a file into a memory buffer buffer. fwrite(buffer, size, count, fptr) writes count items of size bytes each from buffer to a file. Let's illustrate reading and writing using some of these functions:

```
#include <stdio.h>
#include <stdlib.h> // For exit()

int main() {
   FILE *fptr_write, *fptr_read;
   char filename[] = "datafile.txt";
   char data_to_write[] = "This is some text data.\nAnd another line.";
   char buffer[100];
   int number = 123;
   float value = 3.14;

   // Write to file
   fptr_write = fopen(filename, "w");
   if (fptr_write == NULL) {
      perror("Error opening file for writing"); // Error handling using perror
      exit(1);
   }
   fprintf(fptr_write, "Number: %d, Value: %.2f\n", number, value); // Formatted
output
   fputs(data_to_write, fptr_write); // Write string
```

```
    fclose(fptr_write);

    // Read from file
    fptr_read = fopen(filename, "r");
    if (fptr_read == NULL) {
        perror("Error opening file for reading"); // Error handling using perror
        exit(1);
    }

    printf("\nReading from file:\n");
    while (fscanf(fptr_read, "Number: %d, Value: %f", &number, &value) == 2) { //
Formatted input
        printf("Read Number: %d, Value: %.2f\n", number, value);
    }
    while (fgets(buffer, sizeof(buffer), fptr_read) != NULL) { // Line-based input
        printf("%s", buffer);
    }
    fclose(fptr_read);

    return 0;
}
```

This example demonstrates writing formatted data, a string, and then reading back formatted data and lines from a file. It also uses perror() for more informative error messages, discussed in the error handling section below. As Schildt highlights in "C: The Complete Reference" (Schildt, 2000), C's file I/O functions provide a flexible and powerful set of tools for handling various file formats and data processing needs, from simple text files to complex binary data.

File pointers and modes are central to file handling in C. The FILE * type, as returned by fopen(), is a *pointer* to a structure that the C standard library uses to manage the file stream. This structure contains information about the current position in the file, error status, and buffers used for I/O operations. You don't directly manipulate the members of this structure, but you use the FILE * pointer as a handle in file I/O functions. The *file mode* string passed to fopen() dictates how the file will be accessed and manipulated. Let's elaborate on file modes:

1. **"r" (Read):** Opens an existing file for reading. File pointer is positioned at the beginning of the file. If the file does not exist, fopen() returns NULL.
2. **"w" (Write):** Creates a new file for writing. If a file with the same name already exists, it is truncated to zero length (overwritten). File pointer is positioned at the beginning of the file.
3. **"a" (Append):** Opens a file for appending. If the file exists, new data is written at the end of the file. If the file does not exist, a new file is created. File pointer is positioned at the end of the file before each write operation.
4. **"r+" (Read and Write):** Opens an existing file for both reading and writing. File pointer is positioned at the beginning of the file. The file must exist for this mode to succeed.
5. **"w+" (Read and Write):** Creates a new file for both reading and writing. If a file with the same name exists, it is truncated. File pointer is positioned at the beginning of the file.
6. **"a+" (Read and Append):** Opens a file for both reading and appending. If the file exists, writing starts at the end of the file. If the file does not exist, a new file is created. Read access is possible from the beginning of the file.

Adding "b" to any of these modes (e.g., "rb", "wb", "r+b") indicates *binary mode*. In binary mode, data is treated as raw bytes without any text-specific interpretation. In text mode (without "b"), some system-specific translations may occur, such as newline character conversion. Binary mode is essential for handling non-text files like images, executables, or structured data files where byte-for-byte preservation is critical.

Understanding file modes is crucial for correctly specifying the intended file operation and avoiding unexpected behavior. For example, using "w" mode when you intend to append to a file will result in overwriting the existing file content.

Error handling in file operations is paramount for writing robust and reliable programs. File operations are susceptible to various errors: file not found, permission denied, disk full, read/write errors, and more. Ignoring errors can lead to program crashes, data corruption, or unexpected behavior. The primary mechanism for error handling is checking the return values of file I/O functions. fopen() returns NULL on failure. fgetc() and fgets() return EOF on end-of-file or error. fscanf() returns the number of input items successfully matched and assigned, which may be less than expected or EOF in case of error or premature end of file. fprintf(), fputc(), fputs(), fwrite(), fclose() return 0 on success and EOF (or a non-zero value) on error. Checking these return values allows you to detect errors and take appropriate actions, such as displaying error messages, logging errors, or gracefully exiting the program. The perror() function, declared in <stdio.h>, is a useful tool for printing system error messages to the standard error stream (stderr). perror(string) prints the string you provide followed by a system-specific error message describing the last error that occurred. The errno global variable, declared in <errno.h>, stores the error number of the last system call failure. You can use errno to get more specific error codes if needed, although perror() is often sufficient for basic error reporting. Let's enhance the previous example with error handling:

```
#include <stdio.h>
#include <stdlib.h>
#include <errno.h> // For errno
#include <string.h> // For strerror

int main() {
   FILE *fptr;
   char filename[] = "nonexistent_file.txt";
   char buffer[100];

   fptr = fopen(filename, "r"); // Attempt to open a non-existent file in read mode
   if (fptr == NULL) {
      perror("Error opening file"); // Use perror for error message

      printf("errno value: %d\n", errno); // Print errno value
      printf("Error string: %s\n", strerror(errno)); // Use strerror to get error string

      return 1; // Indicate error
   }

   printf("File opened successfully.\n"); // This line will not be reached in this case

   fclose(fptr); // fclose is called only if fopen succeeds. In this case, it won't be
called.

   return 0;
}
```

This example attempts to open a non-existent file in read mode, which will fail. The code checks for NULL return from fopen(), uses perror() to print a descriptive error message, and also demonstrates how to access errno and use strerror() (from <string.h>) to get a textual representation of the error code. Robust error handling is not just about making your program work correctly under normal circumstances; it's about making it resilient and predictable in the face of errors, providing informative feedback to the user or logging system when problems occur. As Maguire stresses in "Writing Solid Code" (Maguire, 1993), meticulous error checking and handling are hallmarks of professional and reliable software development, especially in file handling operations where external factors and system dependencies can introduce potential failure points.

In conclusion, file handling in C is a fundamental skill that enables programs to interact with persistent data, process external inputs, and generate outputs that outlive program execution. Mastering file opening and closing, reading and writing data in various formats, understanding file pointers and modes, and implementing robust error handling are essential for building practical and robust C applications. This chapter has provided a comprehensive introduction to these key aspects of file handling, equipping learners with the knowledge and techniques to effectively integrate file I/O operations into their C programs and bridge the gap between program logic and persistent data storage. The subsequent chapters will build upon these foundations, exploring more advanced C programming concepts and techniques that further enhance your ability to develop sophisticated and powerful applications.

Chapter 13 Advanced Data Structures in C

In this chapter, you will learn the following:

1. Lists and Linked Lists
    a. Array-Based Lists
    b. Sorted Lists (Insertion, Sequential Search, Binary Search, Deletion)
    c. Dynamic Data and Linked Lists (Singly and Doubly Linked Lists)

Lists and Linked Lists: Beyond Simple Arrays

While arrays offer a foundational way to organize collections of data in C, their static nature and limitations in dynamic resizing often necessitate more flexible and adaptable data structures for complex applications. *Advanced data structures*, particularly *lists* and *linked lists*, provide solutions to these challenges, enabling programs to efficiently manage dynamic collections of data that can grow or shrink during runtime. Imagine managing a dynamically changing playlist in a music player, a to-do list that users can expand or contract at will, or a queue of tasks waiting to be processed in an operating system – these scenarios demand data structures capable of adapting to varying data volumes and supporting efficient insertion and deletion of elements without the constraints of fixed-size arrays. This chapter will delve into the concepts of lists, exploring array-based implementations and their inherent limitations, then transitioning to dynamic data structures with a focus on linked lists – both singly and doubly linked – highlighting their advantages in dynamic memory management and efficient manipulation of data collections. Understanding these advanced data structures is not simply about learning new data types; it's about expanding your problem-solving toolkit and mastering techniques for handling dynamic data effectively, crucial for building sophisticated and adaptable C applications.

Lists, in their abstract concept, represent ordered collections of items. In C, lists can be implemented in various ways, with *array-based lists* being a straightforward approach. An array-based list utilizes a standard array to store list elements. Alongside the array itself, you typically maintain a variable to track the *current size* of the list, as the underlying array might be partially filled. *Array-based lists* are simple to implement and provide direct access to elements using array indexing, offering constant-time access to any element given its index. This direct access is a significant advantage when frequent element retrieval by position is needed. However, array-based lists inherit the limitations of arrays: their size is fixed at allocation time (static nature). While you can create a larger array than initially needed and manage a "logical size," expanding the list beyond the array's capacity requires creating a new, larger array, copying all existing elements, and then adding the new element – an operation that can be time-consuming, especially for large lists (Sedgewick & Wayne, 2011). Furthermore, insertion or deletion of elements in the middle of an array-based list is inefficient, requiring shifting subsequent elements to make space or fill gaps, resulting in linear time complexity for these operations. Consider an application like a simple inventory management system where you have a predefined maximum number of items you will ever store. An array-based list could be suitable for storing item names or IDs, allowing for quick retrieval of item information by its index (e.g., item number). However, if the inventory size becomes unpredictable or requires frequent insertions and deletions (items being added or removed frequently), array-based lists become less efficient. Let's illustrate a basic array-based list implementation:

```
#include <stdio.h>
#include <stdlib.h> // For exit()

#define MAX_SIZE 10 // Maximum capacity of the list

int list[MAX_SIZE];
int list_size = 0; // Current size of the list
```

```
// Function to add an element to the end of the list
void add_element(int value) {
    if (list_size >= MAX_SIZE) {
        printf("List is full. Cannot add more elements.\n");
        return;
    }
    list[list_size] = value;
    list_size++;
}

// Function to print the list elements
void print_list() {
    printf("List elements: ");
    for (int i = 0; i < list_size; i++) {
        printf("%d ", list[i]);
    }
    printf("\n");
}

int main() {
    add_element(10);
    add_element(20);
    add_element(30);
    print_list(); // Output: List elements: 10 20 30
    return 0;
}
```

This code demonstrates a rudimentary array-based list with add_element and print_list functions. It highlights the basic operations but also the fixed-size limitation (MAX_SIZE). For situations requiring more dynamic resizing and efficient insertion/deletion, linked lists become a more appropriate choice.

Sorted lists build upon the concept of lists by maintaining their elements in a sorted order, typically based on some key value. Maintaining sorted order enables efficient searching using algorithms like *binary search. Insertion* into a sorted array-based list requires finding the correct position to insert the new element to maintain sorted order and then shifting subsequent elements to make space. *Sequential search* (or linear search) involves iterating through the list from the beginning until the target element is found or the end of the list is reached. For an unsorted list or small lists, sequential search is simple to implement. However, its time complexity is linear (O(n)) in the worst case, as you might have to examine every element. *Binary search*, applicable only to *sorted lists*, significantly improves search efficiency. It works by repeatedly dividing the search interval in half. If the middle element is the target value, the search is successful. If the target value is less than the middle element, the search continues in the left half; otherwise, in the right half. This halving approach reduces the search space exponentially, resulting in a logarithmic time complexity (O(log n)), which is significantly faster than sequential search for large sorted lists (Cormen, Leiserson, Rivest, & Stein, 2009). *Deletion* from a sorted array-based list also requires shifting subsequent elements to close the gap and maintain contiguity. Let's extend the array-based list example to incorporate sorted insertion and search:

```
#include <stdio.h>
#include <stdlib.h>

#define MAX_SIZE 10
int sorted_list[MAX_SIZE];
int sorted_list_size = 0;

// Function to insert into a sorted list, maintaining sorted order
void sorted_insert(int value) {
   if (sorted_list_size >= MAX_SIZE) {
      printf("Sorted list is full. Cannot insert.\n");
      return;
   }
   int i = sorted_list_size - 1;
   // Shift elements to the right to make space for insertion
   while (i >= 0 && sorted_list[i] > value) {
      sorted_list[i + 1] = sorted_list[i];
      i--;
```

```
    }
    sorted_list[i + 1] = value; // Insert the value
    sorted_list_size++;
}

// Binary search function (assuming list is sorted in ascending order)
int binary_search(int value) {
    int low = 0, high = sorted_list_size - 1;
    while (low <= high) {
        int mid = low + (high - low) / 2; // Prevent potential overflow
        if (sorted_list[mid] == value) {
            return mid; // Value found at index mid
        } else if (sorted_list[mid] < value) {
            low = mid + 1; // Search in the right half
        } else {
            high = mid - 1; // Search in the left half
        }
    }
    return -1; // Value not found
}

// ... (print_list function from previous example would also apply here) ...

int main() {
    sorted_insert(30);
    sorted_insert(10);
    sorted_insert(20);
    print_list(); // Output: Sorted list elements: 10 20 30

    int index = binary_search(20);
    if (index != -1) {
        printf("Value 20 found at index %d.\n", index); // Output: Value 20 found at
index 1.
    } else {
        printf("Value 20 not found.\n");
    }
    return 0;
}
```

This extended example demonstrates sorted_insert (maintaining sorted order during insertion) and binary_search functions within an array-based sorted list. Sorted lists and binary search are highly relevant in applications where efficient data lookup is critical, such as phone directories, dictionaries, or search engines (Knuth, 1998).

Dynamic data and linked lists address the limitations of array-based lists by using dynamic memory allocation to create lists that can grow and shrink as needed. *Linked lists* are dynamic data structures composed of *nodes*. Each *node* in a linked list contains two primary components: *data* (the actual data value being stored) and a *pointer* (or link) to the *next node* in the sequence. The nodes are linked together using these pointers, forming a chain. The last node in the list typically has its pointer set to NULL to indicate the end of the list. The first node in the list is called the *head* of the list, and you access the list through a pointer to the head node.

Singly linked lists are the simplest form of linked lists, where each node has a pointer only to the *next* node. *Insertion* and *deletion* in a singly linked list can be performed efficiently at any position, particularly at the beginning or in the middle, as it mainly involves pointer adjustments without the need to shift large blocks of memory as in array-based lists. However, accessing an element at a specific position in a singly linked list requires traversing the list from the head, which is a sequential process and can be time-consuming for long lists (linear time complexity for access by index). *Traversal* in a singly linked list is unidirectional – you can only move from the head to the tail, following the next pointers. Let's illustrate a singly linked list implementation:

```
#include <stdio.h>
#include <stdlib.h>

// Node structure for singly linked list
struct Node {
   int data;
   struct Node *next; // Pointer to the next node
};

struct Node* head = NULL; // Head of the linked list (initially empty)
```

```
// Function to insert a node at the beginning of the linked list
void insert_at_beginning(int data) {
    struct Node *newNode = (struct Node*)malloc(sizeof(struct Node));
    if (newNode == NULL) {
        fprintf(stderr, "Memory allocation failed!\n");
        exit(1);
    }
    newNode->data = data;
    newNode->next = head; // New node points to the current head
    head = newNode;      // Update head to the new node
}

// Function to print the linked list
void print_linked_list() {
    struct Node *current = head;
    printf("Linked list: ");
    while (current != NULL) {
        printf("%d -> ", current->data);
        current = current->next; // Move to the next node
    }
    printf("NULL\n");
}

int main() {
    insert_at_beginning(30);
    insert_at_beginning(20);
    insert_at_beginning(10);
    print_linked_list(); // Output: Linked list: 10 -> 20 -> 30 -> NULL
    return 0;
}
```

This code provides a basic singly linked list with insert_at_beginning and print_linked_list functions. It demonstrates dynamic memory allocation for nodes using malloc and pointer manipulation to link nodes together. Singly linked lists are suitable for implementing stacks, queues, and representing dynamic sequences where frequent insertions and deletions are performed, such as managing a browser history or a task queue.

Doubly linked lists enhance singly linked lists by adding a pointer in each node to the *previous* node, in addition to the pointer to the *next* node. This bidirectional linking allows for traversal in both forward and backward directions and simplifies certain operations, particularly *deletion from the middle* of the list. In a singly linked list, to delete a node in the middle, you need to traverse to the node *before* the node to be deleted to adjust its next pointer. In a doubly linked list, you can directly access the previous node using the prev pointer of the node to be deleted, making deletion from the middle more efficient. However, doubly linked lists require more memory per node (to store the extra prev pointer) and slightly more complex insertion and deletion operations due to the need to update both next and prev pointers. Undo/redo functionality in text editors or navigation through a music playlist with "previous" and "next" buttons are real-world scenarios where doubly linked lists are often employed, as they benefit from bidirectional traversal and efficient deletion from arbitrary positions. Let's extend the previous example to a doubly linked list:

```
#include <stdio.h>
#include <stdlib.h>

// Node structure for doubly linked list
struct Node {
    int data;
    struct Node *next; // Pointer to the next node
    struct Node *prev; // Pointer to the previous node (added for doubly linked list)
};

struct Node* head = NULL; // Head of the doubly linked list (initially empty)
struct Node* tail = NULL; // Tail of the doubly linked list (initially empty)

// Function to insert a node at the beginning of the doubly linked list
void insert_at_beginning_doubly(int data) {
    struct Node *newNode = (struct Node*)malloc(sizeof(struct Node));
    if (newNode == NULL) {
        fprintf(stderr, "Memory allocation failed!\n");
        exit(1);
    }
    newNode->data = data;
    newNode->prev = NULL; // New node is at the beginning, so no previous node
    newNode->next = head; // New node's next points to the current head
```

```
    if (head != NULL) {
        head->prev = newNode; // Current head's previous now points to the new
node
    } else {
        tail = newNode; // If list was empty, new node is also the tail
    }
    head = newNode; // Update head to the new node

    if (tail == NULL) { // Handle empty list case initially - if head was null, tail needs
to be set.
        tail = head;  // if head is now set and tail was null, then tail should also be head
as it is single node list.
    }
}


// Function to print the doubly linked list (forward traversal)
void print_doubly_linked_list_forward() {
    struct Node *current = head;
    printf("Doubly linked list (forward): ");
    while (current != NULL) {
        printf("%d <-> ", current->data);
        current = current->next;
    }
    printf("NULL\n");
}

int main() {
    insert_at_beginning_doubly(30);
    insert_at_beginning_doubly(20);
    insert_at_beginning_doubly(10);
    print_doubly_linked_list_forward(); // Output: Doubly linked list (forward): 10 <-
> 20 <-> 30 <-> NULL
    return 0;
}
```

This example demonstrates a basic doubly linked list with insert_at_beginning_doubly and print_doubly_linked_list_forward functions. It highlights the addition of the prev pointer and the necessary pointer adjustments for insertion in a doubly linked list.

Common challenges with linked lists, particularly dynamic memory allocation, include *memory leaks* if dynamically allocated nodes are not properly deallocated using free() when no longer needed. *Pointer errors,* such as null pointer dereferencing (accessing memory through a NULL pointer) and dangling pointers (pointers pointing to memory that has already been freed), are also potential pitfalls. Careful memory management, thorough error checking (e.g., checking malloc() return values), and meticulous pointer manipulation are essential for robust linked list implementations. Tools like memory debuggers (e.g., Valgrind) can be invaluable for detecting memory leaks and pointer errors in C programs using dynamic memory allocation. As Tanenbaum, Augenstein, and Langsam emphasize in "Data Structures Using C" (Tanenbaum, Augenstein, & Langsam, 1990), proper memory management is paramount when working with dynamic data structures like linked lists, and diligent coding practices are crucial to avoid memory-related issues.

In conclusion, advanced data structures like lists and linked lists offer powerful tools for managing dynamic collections of data in C, overcoming the limitations of static arrays. Array-based lists provide simplicity and direct access but suffer from fixed size and inefficient insertions/deletions. Sorted lists enhance search efficiency using algorithms like binary search. Linked lists, both singly and doubly linked, offer dynamic resizing and efficient insertion/deletion at the cost of sequential access and increased complexity in pointer management. Choosing the appropriate data structure depends on the specific application requirements, considering factors like data size variability, frequency of insertions/deletions, search operations, and memory constraints. Mastering these advanced data structures, particularly linked lists and dynamic memory allocation, is a crucial step towards building sophisticated and adaptable C programs that can handle complex data management tasks effectively. The subsequent chapters will further explore advanced C programming techniques and build upon these data structure foundations, demonstrating their application in real-world scenarios.

Chapter 14 Object-Oriented Concepts in C (Using Structs and Function Pointers)

In this chapter, you will learn the following:

1. Abstract Data Types
2. Encapsulation in C
3. Function Pointers for Polymorphism

Embracing Abstraction and Flexibility

While C is fundamentally a procedural programming language, its flexible nature and powerful features allow programmers to emulate several core principles of object-oriented programming (OOP). Though C lacks built-in object-oriented constructs like classes and inheritance in the way languages like C++ or Java do, understanding how to apply OOP concepts within C provides significant benefits. It promotes modular design, enhances code reusability, and improves the maintainability of larger C projects, especially as software systems become increasingly complex. This chapter explores how to leverage C's structs and function pointers to approximate key OOP concepts like abstract data types, encapsulation, and polymorphism. It is crucial to understand that this is *emulation*, not true object-oriented programming in the class-based sense. However, adopting these techniques in C allows programmers to build more structured and adaptable code, drawing inspiration from OOP principles even within a procedural paradigm. Mastering these techniques is not about transforming C into an object-oriented language, but rather about expanding your C programming toolkit with powerful design patterns that enhance code organization and flexibility, skills highly valuable in diverse areas from embedded systems to system-level programming.

Abstract Data Types (ADTs) are a cornerstone of software design, focusing on defining data structures based on their behavior (operations) rather than their concrete implementation details. An ADT specifies *what* operations can be performed on the data and *what properties* these operations guarantee, without revealing *how* the data is stored or *how* the operations are implemented. This separation of interface from implementation is key to abstraction, allowing programmers to use data structures without needing to delve into their internal complexities. In C, structures (structs) can be used to effectively represent ADTs. By combining data members (representing the state of the ADT) within a struct and providing functions that operate on these structs (representing the operations of the ADT), we can create abstract data types. The structure definition acts as the public interface, defining the data attributes, while the functions provide the operations defined by the ADT. Consider the classic example of a *Stack* ADT. A stack is characterized by its Last-In, First-Out (LIFO) behavior, with operations like push (add an element to the top), pop (remove and return the top element), peek (view the top element without removing), and isEmpty (check if the stack is empty). We can represent a Stack ADT in C using a structure and functions that operate on it:

```
#include <stdio.h>
#include <stdlib.h> // For malloc, free

// Define the Stack ADT using a struct
typedef struct {
    int *items;    // Pointer to dynamically allocated array to store stack items
    int top;       // Index of the top element (-1 for empty stack)
    int capacity;  // Maximum capacity of the stack
} Stack;

// Function to initialize a Stack
Stack* createStack(int capacity) {
    Stack* s = (Stack*)malloc(sizeof(Stack));
    if (!s) {
        fprintf(stderr, "Memory allocation failed for Stack!\n");
        exit(1);
    }
    s->capacity = capacity;
    s->top = -1; // Initialize top to -1 for an empty stack
    s->items = (int*)malloc(s->capacity * sizeof(int));
    if (!s->items) {
        fprintf(stderr, "Memory allocation failed for Stack items!\n");
```

```
        free(s); // Free stack structure if items allocation fails
        exit(1);
    }
    return s;
}

// Function to check if the Stack is empty
int isEmpty(Stack* s) {
    return s->top == -1;
}

// Function to check if the Stack is full
int isFull(Stack* s) {
    return s->top == s->capacity - 1;
}

// Function to push an element onto the Stack
void push(Stack* s, int item) {
    if (isFull(s)) {
        printf("Stack Overflow!\n");
        return;
    }
    s->items[++s->top] = item; // Increment top and then push
    printf("Pushed %d to stack\n", item);
}

// Function to pop an element from the Stack
int pop(Stack* s) {
    if (isEmpty(s)) {
        printf("Stack Underflow!\n");
        return -1; // Or handle error appropriately, e.g., return a special value or signal
error differently
    }
    return s->items[s->top--]; // Return top element and then decrement top
}

// Function to peek at the top element of the Stack
int peek(Stack* s) {
    if (isEmpty(s)) {
        printf("Stack is empty, cannot peek.\n");
        return -1; // Or handle error appropriately
    }
    return s->items[s->top];
}

int main() {
    Stack* myStack = createStack(5); // Create a stack with capacity 5

    push(myStack, 10);
```

```
    push(myStack, 20);
    push(myStack, 30);

    printf("Top element of stack: %d\n", peek(myStack)); // Output: Top element of
stack: 30

    printf("Popped element: %d\n", pop(myStack));     // Output: Popped element: 30
    printf("Popped element: %d\n", pop(myStack));     // Output: Popped element: 20

    printf("Is stack empty? %s\n", isEmpty(myStack) ? "Yes" : "No"); // Output: Is
stack empty? No

    // ... (Remember to free dynamically allocated memory when done with the stack)
...

    return 0;
}
```

This code example demonstrates how a Stack structure can be defined in C to encapsulate the data (items, top, capacity) and operations (createStack, isEmpty, isFull, push, pop, peek) of a Stack ADT. Users of this Stack ADT interact only through these defined functions, unaware of the underlying array implementation. This aligns with the principles of abstract data types, hiding implementation details and focusing on the interface and behavior. As Liskov and Guttag explain in "Program Development in Java" (Liskov & Guttag, 2001), abstraction is a key principle for managing complexity in software, and ADTs are a fundamental tool for achieving abstraction by separating interface from implementation.

Encapsulation in OOP refers to bundling data (attributes) and methods (functions) that operate on that data within a single unit (an object or class) and controlling access to the internal data, typically through access modifiers (like public, private, protected in languages like C++ or Java). While C structs do not inherently enforce access control like private members, we can achieve *encapsulation in C* by convention and careful design. By declaring the data members within a structure and providing functions that are the *only* way to access and modify this data, we can control how the structure's data is interacted with from outside. This approach, often called *data hiding*, is a form of encapsulation achieved through design principles rather than language enforcement in C. The Stack ADT example above already illustrates a degree of encapsulation. The internal representation of the stack (the items array, top, capacity) is accessed and manipulated *only* through the provided functions (push, pop, etc.). External code interacts with the stack *only* through these functions, not directly manipulating the struct members. To strengthen encapsulation, we can further limit direct access to the struct definition itself by placing the structure definition in a header file but keeping the implementations of the functions in a separate source file. This separation of interface (header file with struct definition and function declarations) from implementation (source file with function definitions) is a key technique for encapsulation in C. Consider a simplified example of a 'Counter' object in C, aiming for encapsulation:

```
// counter.h (Header file - Interface)
#ifndef COUNTER_H
#define COUNTER_H

typedef struct Counter Counter; // Forward declaration of struct Counter

Counter* createCounter();
void incrementCounter(Counter* c);
int getCounterValue(Counter* c);
void destroyCounter(Counter* c);

#endif // COUNTER_H

// counter.c (Source file - Implementation)
#include "counter.h"
#include <stdlib.h>
```

```
struct Counter { // Actual definition of struct Counter (hidden from direct external
access)
    int count;
};

Counter* createCounter() {
    Counter* c = (Counter*)malloc(sizeof(Counter));
    if (!c) {
        fprintf(stderr, "Memory allocation failed for Counter!\n");
        exit(1);
    }
    c->count = 0; // Initialize counter to 0
    return c;
}

void incrementCounter(Counter* c) {
    c->count++;
}

int getCounterValue(Counter* c) {
    return c->count;
}

void destroyCounter(Counter* c) {
    free(c);
}

// main.c (Example usage)
#include <stdio.h>
#include "counter.h"

int main() {
    Counter* myCounter = createCounter();
    incrementCounter(myCounter);
    incrementCounter(myCounter);
    printf("Counter value: %d\n", getCounterValue(myCounter)); // Output: Counter
value: 2
    destroyCounter(myCounter);
    return 0;
}
```

In this example, the structure definition of Counter is placed in counter.c and is not directly exposed in counter.h. counter.h only contains a *forward declaration* (typedef struct Counter Counter;) and function prototypes. Users of the Counter module in main.c include counter.h and can use the functions (createCounter, incrementCounter, getCounterValue, destroyCounter) to interact with a Counter object but do not have direct access to the internal count member. This exemplifies encapsulation in C through information hiding and controlled access via functions. As McConnell argues in "Code Complete" (McConnell, 2004), encapsulation is vital for creating modular and maintainable code, reducing dependencies between different parts of the program and making code easier to understand, modify, and test.

Function pointers in C are variables that can hold the address of a function. They enable *polymorphism* – the ability to perform different actions based on the actual type of object or data being handled, even when accessed through a common interface. In the context of OOP, polymorphism allows objects of different classes to respond differently to the same method call. In C, we can emulate polymorphism using function pointers within structures. By including a function pointer member in a structure, we can associate different function implementations with different structure instances or types. Consider a scenario of handling different *Shape* types (e.g., Circle, Square, Triangle), each having a draw operation, but the implementation of draw is different for each shape. We can define a generic Shape structure with a function pointer draw and then create specific shape structures (Circle, Square, Triangle) that embed the Shape structure and associate their specific draw implementations with the draw function pointer of the embedded Shape. This allows us to call a generic draw function pointer on any Shape pointer, and the correct, shape-specific draw implementation will be executed at runtime (dynamic dispatch). Let's illustrate polymorphism with a Shape example in C:

```
#include <stdio.h>
#include <stdlib.h>
#include <math.h> // For M_PI

// Define a generic Shape structure with a function pointer for draw
typedef struct Shape {
   void (*draw)(struct Shape*); // Function pointer to a draw function
   // ... common shape properties can be added here if needed ...
} Shape;

// Define Circle structure, embedding Shape
typedef struct Circle {
   Shape base; // Embed the generic Shape structure
   float radius;
} Circle;

// Define Square structure, embedding Shape
typedef struct Square {
   Shape base; // Embed the generic Shape structure
   float side;
} Square;

// Draw function for Circle
void drawCircle(Shape* shape) {
   Circle* circle = (Circle*)shape; // Cast Shape pointer to Circle pointer
   printf("Drawing Circle with radius: %.2f\n", circle->radius);
   // ... (Actual circle drawing code would go here) ...
}

// Draw function for Square
void drawSquare(Shape* shape) {
   Square* square = (Square*)shape; // Cast Shape pointer to Square pointer
   printf("Drawing Square with side: %.2f\n", square->side);
   // ... (Actual square drawing code would go here) ...
}

// Function to create a Circle object
Circle* createCircle(float radius) {
   Circle* c = (Circle*)malloc(sizeof(Circle));
   if (!c) {
      fprintf(stderr, "Memory allocation failed for Circle!\n");
      exit(1);
   }
   c->base.draw = drawCircle; // Assign Circle's draw function to Shape's function
pointer
   c->radius = radius;
   return c;
}
```

```
// Function to create a Square object
Square* createSquare(float side) {
    Square* s = (Square*)malloc(sizeof(Square));
    if (!s) {
        fprintf(stderr, "Memory allocation failed for Square!\n");
        exit(1);
    }
    s->base.draw = drawSquare; // Assign Square's draw function to Shape's function
pointer
    s->side = side;
    return s;
}

int main() {
    Shape* shapes[2]; // Array of Shape pointers

    shapes[0] = (Shape*)createCircle(5.0); // Store Circle pointer in Shape array
    shapes[1] = (Shape*)createSquare(4.0);  // Store Square pointer in Shape array

    for (int i = 0; i < 2; i++) {
        shapes[i]->draw(shapes[i]); // Call the draw function through the function
pointer
    }
    // Output:
    // Drawing Circle with radius: 5.0
    // Drawing Square with side: 4.0

    // ... (Remember to free dynamically allocated memory for shapes) ...

    return 0;
}
```

In this example, Shape structure contains a function pointer draw. Circle and Square structures embed the Shape structure. createCircle and createSquare functions create Circle and Square objects and crucially *assign the specific draw functions (drawCircle and drawSquare) to the draw function pointer* of the embedded Shape base. In main(), when shapes[i]->draw(shapes[i]) is called, the correct drawCircle or drawSquare function is invoked based on the actual type of the shape pointed to by shapes[i], achieving polymorphism through function pointers. As Gamma, Helm, Johnson, and Vlissides detail in "Design Patterns: Elements of Reusable Object-Oriented

Software" (Gamma et al., 1994), polymorphism is a fundamental design pattern in OOP that enhances flexibility and extensibility by allowing code to work with objects of different classes in a uniform way through a shared interface. While C's function pointer approach to polymorphism is more manual than class-based polymorphism in OOP languages, it provides a powerful mechanism for achieving similar dynamic behavior and code flexibility within the C paradigm.

In conclusion, while C is not inherently object-oriented, it provides sufficient tools – structs and function pointers – to emulate core OOP concepts like abstract data types, encapsulation, and polymorphism. By carefully designing structures to represent ADTs, employing data hiding techniques for encapsulation, and utilizing function pointers for polymorphism, C programmers can adopt object-oriented design principles to build more structured, modular, and maintainable C programs, particularly for larger and more complex software systems. Understanding these techniques enhances a C programmer's ability to manage code complexity, improve reusability, and create more adaptable and extensible applications, drawing valuable lessons from OOP even within the procedural C paradigm. The next chapters will build upon these foundations, exploring further advanced C programming techniques and demonstrating how these concepts are applied in more complex and practical programming scenarios.

© 2025 Mark John Lado

Chapter 15 Implementing Windows Form-based GUI in C (Optional, if using WinAPI or GTK+)

In this chapter, you will learn the following:

1. Introduction to Windows Programming in C
2. Creating a Simple GUI Application
3. Event-Driven Programming in C

Interfacing with the Graphical World

While C is often celebrated for its efficiency and low-level control, particularly in system and embedded programming, it's also capable of creating graphical user interfaces (GUIs). Though not as straightforward as in languages specifically designed for GUI development (like C# or Java with dedicated frameworks), implementing GUIs in C, especially for Windows, offers a valuable learning experience, providing deep insights into operating system interaction and event-driven programming. This chapter, while optional in the broader context of C fundamentals, delves into the principles of creating Windows form-based GUIs directly in C, primarily using the native Windows API (WinAPI). While libraries like GTK+ offer cross-platform GUI development in C, focusing on WinAPI provides a more direct understanding of Windows-specific GUI paradigms and is often more relevant for those working within the Windows ecosystem or aiming for a deeper understanding of Windows internals. Embarking on Windows GUI programming in C is not merely about creating visually appealing applications; it's about mastering a lower-level approach to GUI creation, understanding the event-driven model, and appreciating the intricacies of operating system interfaces, skills that are highly valuable for system programmers, embedded systems developers working with Windows-based platforms, or anyone seeking a comprehensive understanding of the computing stack.

Introduction to Windows Programming in C fundamentally means working with the Windows API (Application Programming Interface). WinAPI is a vast collection of functions, data structures, and protocols provided by Microsoft Windows that allows developers to interact directly with the operating system and its functionalities, including window management, graphics, input handling, and much more. Windows GUI applications are fundamentally *event-driven*. This means the program's flow is not linear but rather reacts to *events* – user actions like mouse clicks and keyboard presses, or system events like window resizing and repaint requests. The core of a Windows GUI application is the *Window Procedure* (often called WindowProc or WndProc). This is a function you define that the operating system calls whenever an *event* (represented as a *message*) occurs for a specific window in your application. Each window in Windows is identified by a unique *Window Handle* (HWND), which is essentially a numerical identifier that the system uses to refer to a window. When an event occurs for a window, Windows sends a *message* to the window's associated WindowProc. This message is typically an integer value (like WM_PAINT for a repaint request, WM_LBUTTONDOWN for a left mouse button press). The WindowProc then examines the message and performs the appropriate actions based on the event. This message-driven architecture is the foundation of all Windows GUI applications, from simple dialog boxes to complex desktop applications (Petzold, 1998). To begin Windows programming in C, you will primarily interact with the <windows.h> header file, which declares the essential WinAPI functions, data types, and constants necessary for building Windows applications.

Creating a Simple GUI Application in C using WinAPI, even a basic one, involves several key steps. Let's outline the creation of a minimal window that simply displays "Hello, Windows!" in its client area.

1. **Include Header File:** Start by including the <windows.h> header file in your C source code: #include <windows.h>. This provides access to all the necessary WinAPI definitions.
2. **Define the Window Procedure (WindowProc):** This

function is the heart of your window's behavior. It must conform to a specific signature defined by WinAPI. A basic WindowProc structure is as follows:

```
LRESULT CALLBACK WindowProc(HWND hwnd, UINT uMsg,
WPARAM wParam, LPARAM lParam) {
   switch (uMsg) {
      case WM_PAINT: { // Handle repaint message
         PAINTSTRUCT ps;
         HDC hdc = BeginPaint(hwnd, &ps); // Get device context for
drawing
         RECT rect;
         GetClientRect(hwnd, &rect); // Get client area rectangle
         DrawText(hdc, "Hello, Windows!", -1, &rect, DT_CENTER |
DT_VCENTER | DT_SINGLELINE); // Draw text
         EndPaint(hwnd, &ps); // End painting
         return 0;
      }
      case WM_DESTROY: { // Handle window destruction message
         PostQuitMessage(0); // Post a quit message to the message queue
         return 0;
      }
      default:
         return DefWindowProc(hwnd, uMsg, wParam, lParam); // Default
message processing
   }
}
```

- LRESULT CALLBACK WindowProc(...): This is the function signature required by WinAPI for window procedures. LRESULT is a type for message result values, CALLBACK is a calling convention specifier. HWND hwnd is the window handle, UINT uMsg is the message ID, WPARAM wParam and LPARAM lParam are message parameters.
- switch (uMsg): A switch statement to handle different messages.
- WM_PAINT: Message sent when the window needs to

be repainted (e.g., initially shown, resized, or covered and uncovered).

- BeginPaint(hwnd, &ps) and EndPaint(hwnd, &ps): Functions to prepare for and finalize painting in the window. PAINTSTRUCT contains painting information. HDC hdc is a *Device Context Handle*, used for drawing operations.
- GetClientRect(hwnd, &rect): Gets the rectangle representing the window's client area (the area where you can draw).
- DrawText(hdc, "Hello, Windows!", -1, &rect, DT_CENTER | DT_VCENTER | DT_SINGLELINE): WinAPI function to draw text in a rectangle. DT_CENTER, DT_VCENTER, DT_SINGLELINE are flags to center the text horizontally and vertically and draw it as a single line.
- WM_DESTROY: Message sent when the window is being destroyed (closed).
- PostQuitMessage(0): Posts a WM_QUIT message to the application's message queue, signaling the message loop to terminate.
- DefWindowProc(hwnd, uMsg, wParam, lParam): Default window message processing function. For messages your WindowProc doesn't explicitly handle, you should call DefWindowProc to let Windows handle them in the default way.

1. **Define WinMain Function:** The entry point for a Windows GUI application is WinMain instead of main. WinMain is specific to Windows GUI applications and handles initialization, window creation, message loop, and application termination.

```
int WINAPI WinMain(HINSTANCE hInstance, HINSTANCE
hPrevInstance, LPSTR lpCmdLine, int nCmdShow) {
   const char CLASS_NAME[] = "SampleWindowClass"; // Window class
name

   WNDCLASS wc = { }; // Window class structure

   wc.lpfnWndProc  = WindowProc; // Set window procedure
   wc.hInstance    = hInstance;  // Instance handle of the application
   wc.lpszClassName = CLASS_NAME; // Class name

   RegisterClass(&wc); // Register the window class

   HWND hwnd = CreateWindowEx( // Create the window
      0,                    // Optional window styles.
      CLASS_NAME,                // Window class name
      "Sample Window",           // Window title text
      WS_OVERLAPPEDWINDOW | WS_VISIBLE, // Window styles:
overlapped, resizable, visible
      CW_USEDEFAULT, CW_USEDEFAULT, CW_USEDEFAULT,
CW_USEDEFAULT, // Default position and size
      NULL,      // Parent window   (no parent)
      NULL,      // Menu            (no menu)
      hInstance, // Instance handle
      NULL       // Pointer not to window-creation data
   );

   if (hwnd == NULL) {
      return 0; // Window creation failed
   }

   ShowWindow(hwnd, nCmdShow); // Show the window
   UpdateWindow(hwnd);        // Update the window (force WM_PAINT)


   MSG msg; // Message structure
   // Message loop
   while (GetMessage(&msg, NULL, 0, 0) > 0) { // Get messages from the
message queue
```

```
        TranslateMessage(&msg); // Translate virtual-key messages into
character messages
        DispatchMessage(&msg);  // Dispatch message to WindowProc
    }

    return 0; // Application exit code (from PostQuitMessage)
}
```

- int WINAPI WinMain(...): WINAPI specifies the Windows API calling convention. HINSTANCE hInstance is the *instance handle* of the application (unique identifier). HINSTANCE hPrevInstance is always NULL in modern Windows. LPSTR lpCmdLine is the command-line string. int nCmdShow specifies how the window should be initially shown (e.g., normal, minimized, maximized).
- WNDCLASS wc = { };: WNDCLASS structure defines the properties of a *window class*. A window class is a template for creating windows.
- wc.lpfnWndProc = WindowProc;: Assigns the WindowProc function to handle messages for windows of this class.
- wc.hInstance = hInstance;: Sets the instance handle.
- wc.lpszClassName = CLASS_NAME;: Sets the class name.
- RegisterClass(&wc): Registers the window class with the operating system.
- CreateWindowEx(...): Creates an *instance* of the window class – the actual window. It takes parameters like extended styles, class name, window title, window styles (WS_OVERLAPPEDWINDOW | WS_VISIBLE for a typical resizable window), position, size, parent window (NULL for top-level window), menu (NULL for no menu), instance

handle, and creation data (NULL in this case). Returns the HWND of the created window.

- ShowWindow(hwnd, nCmdShow): Makes the window visible on the screen based on nCmdShow.
- UpdateWindow(hwnd): Forces a WM_PAINT message to be sent to the WindowProc to initially paint the window.
- MSG msg;: MSG structure is used to store message information retrieved from the message queue.
- **Message Loop:** while (GetMessage(&msg, NULL, 0, 0) > 0): The core message loop. GetMessage() retrieves messages from the application's message queue. It blocks until a message is available (except for WM_QUIT). TranslateMessage(&msg) translates virtual-key messages into character messages (e.g., for keyboard input). DispatchMessage(&msg) dispatches the message to the appropriate WindowProc function for handling based on the window handle in the message. The loop continues until GetMessage() returns 0, which happens when a WM_QUIT message is received (usually via PostQuitMessage).

2. **Compile and Run:** Compile this C code using a Windows C compiler (like MinGW or Visual Studio's compiler) and link against the necessary libraries (typically, no explicit linking is needed for this basic example as kernel32.lib, user32.lib, and gdi32.lib are linked by default in many C compiler setups for Windows). Running the executable will display a simple window with "Hello, Windows!" in the center.

Event-Driven Programming in C using WinAPI is entirely centered around *messages* and the *Window Procedure.* The flow of control in your GUI application is dictated by the messages that Windows sends to your window. Windows sends messages in response to:

- **User Input:** Mouse clicks, mouse movements, keyboard presses, menu selections. Each user action generates one or more messages. For example, a mouse click can generate WM_LBUTTONDOWN, WM_LBUTTONUP, WM_MOUSEMOVE messages. Key presses generate WM_KEYDOWN, WM_KEYUP, WM_CHAR messages.
- **System Events:** Window creation (WM_CREATE), window destruction (WM_DESTROY), window resizing (WM_SIZE), window repaint requests (WM_PAINT), window activation/deactivation (WM_ACTIVATE), timer events (WM_TIMER), and many more.

Your WindowProc acts as the *central event handler.* It's a callback function that Windows calls to notify your application about events related to a specific window. The uMsg parameter of WindowProc identifies the type of event (the message ID). wParam and lParam provide message-specific parameters, often containing information about mouse coordinates, key codes, window dimensions, etc. The switch statement within WindowProc is crucial for *message dispatching.* Each case in the switch handles a specific message type (e.g., WM_PAINT, WM_DESTROY, WM_LBUTTONDOWN). For each message type, you write the code to respond to that event. For instance, in WM_PAINT, you write the code to redraw the window's contents. In WM_LBUTTONDOWN, you might write code to process a mouse click on a button or initiate some action based on the click coordinates. If your WindowProc doesn't handle a particular message, you *must* call DefWindowProc to allow Windows to process the message in a default manner. Ignoring messages or not calling DefWindowProc for unhandled messages can lead to incorrect window behavior or application instability.

Common Challenges and Considerations:

- **Complexity of WinAPI:** WinAPI is vast and can be overwhelming for beginners. The sheer number of functions, structures, and constants can be daunting. Start with simple examples and gradually explore more advanced features. Resources like the official Microsoft documentation (MSDN/Microsoft Learn) and Charles Petzold's "Programming Windows" (Petzold, 1998) are invaluable for learning WinAPI.
- **Boilerplate Code:** Windows GUI programming in raw C/WinAPI often involves a significant amount of boilerplate code, even for simple applications (window registration, message loop setup, basic window procedure structure). This can be verbose compared to higher-level GUI frameworks. For more complex applications, consider using GUI frameworks built on top of WinAPI (like MFC, though less common now) or cross-platform frameworks like GTK+ (if portability is required) which provide higher levels of abstraction and reduce boilerplate.
- **Memory Management:** As with all C programming, manual memory management is crucial in WinAPI GUI applications. You are responsible for allocating and freeing resources like window handles, device contexts, brushes, pens, bitmaps, and any dynamically allocated memory you use within your application. Failure to manage memory properly can lead to memory leaks and resource exhaustion.
- **Debugging:** Debugging event-driven GUI applications can

be more complex than debugging linear console applications. Use debuggers effectively to step through your WindowProc and observe message flow. Tools like Spy++ (included with Visual Studio) can be helpful for monitoring Windows messages sent to your application.

- **Resource Management (Beyond Memory):** Windows GUI applications often use resources like icons, cursors, menus, dialogs, and strings. These are typically managed as *resources* within the application's executable file. WinAPI provides functions to load and use these resources. Resource management adds another layer of complexity to Windows GUI programming.

Real-World Relevance and Educational Value

While C/WinAPI is not the most common choice for rapid application development of modern desktop GUIs, understanding Windows GUI programming in C using WinAPI remains highly valuable:

- **System Programming and OS Internals:** It provides an unparalleled understanding of how Windows GUI subsystems work at a lower level. This knowledge is invaluable for system programmers, driver developers, and anyone needing to deeply understand Windows internals.
- **Legacy Systems and Maintenance:** A significant amount of existing Windows software is written in C or C++ using WinAPI. Maintaining or extending these legacy systems often requires expertise in WinAPI programming.
- **Embedded Systems and Specialized Applications:** In certain embedded systems scenarios or for very performance-critical, resource-constrained Windows applications, direct WinAPI programming in C might still be a relevant and efficient choice.
- **Educational Value:** Learning WinAPI in C forces you to grapple with fundamental GUI programming concepts (event-driven model, message handling, window management) at a very explicit level, providing a strong foundation for understanding GUI programming principles in general, regardless of the specific framework or language.

In conclusion, implementing Windows form-based GUIs directly in C using WinAPI is a challenging but highly rewarding endeavor. While perhaps not the most practical approach for all modern GUI development, it provides an unparalleled educational experience, fostering a deep understanding of Windows operating system interaction, event-driven programming paradigms, and lower-level GUI principles. By mastering these techniques, you gain valuable skills applicable not only to Windows-specific development but also to broader software engineering principles related to system interaction, event handling, and efficient resource management, skills highly prized in the field of computer technology. For further exploration, delving into more advanced WinAPI features, resource management, custom control creation, and perhaps comparing WinAPI to cross-platform GUI frameworks like GTK+ would be valuable next steps in expanding your GUI programming knowledge in C.

© 2025 Mark John Lado

Chapter 16 Inheritance and Polymorphism in C (Using Function Pointers and Structs)

In this chapter, you will learn the following:

1. Simulating Object-Oriented Programming in C
2. Inheritance-like Behavior in C
3. Polymorphism using Function Pointers

Simulating Object-Oriented Power

Building upon the concepts of abstract data types and encapsulation introduced in the previous chapter, this chapter delves into the more advanced object-oriented principles of *inheritance* and *polymorphism* within the procedural landscape of C. While C lacks the direct language constructs for these features found in languages like C++ or Java, clever use of structs and function pointers allows us to approximate their behavior, achieving code reusability and flexibility often associated with OOP paradigms. It's crucial to reiterate that we are *simulating* OOP, not transforming C into an object-oriented language; rather, we are leveraging C's inherent capabilities to adopt design patterns inspired by OOP, enhancing code organization and adaptability, particularly in larger, more complex C projects. This chapter will explore how struct composition can mimic inheritance-like relationships and how function pointers serve as the linchpin for achieving polymorphism in C, equipping learners with the techniques to introduce object-oriented design principles into their C code, even within a procedural context.

Simulating Object-Oriented Programming in C is a practice driven by the desire to structure and organize C code in a more modular, reusable, and maintainable way, often drawing inspiration from the proven benefits of OOP design. In essence, we aim to achieve the *spirit* of OOP – abstraction, encapsulation, inheritance, and polymorphism – using the tools C provides: structs, function pointers, and disciplined coding conventions. We are not trying to force C to become an object-oriented language; instead, we are applying OOP *design principles* within the confines of the C language. This approach can be particularly beneficial in large C projects where code organization, modularity, and extensibility become critical. By using structs to represent data and function pointers to represent methods (operations), we can create structures that behave much like objects in OOP languages. The key takeaway is that while C lacks language-level support for classes and inheritance, the core ideas of OOP – abstraction, encapsulation (as explored in Chapter 14), and now inheritance and polymorphism – can be effectively *modeled* and *achieved* through careful C programming practices (Stevens, 2005).

Achieving *inheritance-like behavior in C* often relies on struct *composition* or *embedding*. In true OOP languages, inheritance allows a class to inherit properties and behaviors from a parent class, establishing an "is-a" relationship. In C, we can mimic this by embedding one struct (representing the "base class") within another struct (representing the "derived class"). The embedded struct effectively becomes a member of the outer struct, giving the outer struct access to the members of the embedded struct. Let's consider a real-world scenario: representing different types of vehicles, such as cars and motorcycles, inheriting from a generic Vehicle type. A Vehicle might have common properties like engine_size and num_wheels. Car and Motorcycle would *inherit* these general vehicle properties but also have their own specific attributes (e.g., Car might have num_doors, Motorcycle might have has_sidecar). In C, we can structure this as follows:

```
#include <stdio.h>
#include <stdlib.h>
#include <string.h> // For strcpy

// Base struct: Vehicle
typedef struct Vehicle {
    char model[50];
    int engine_size;
} Vehicle;
```

```
// Derived struct: Car (embedding Vehicle)
typedef struct Car {
    Vehicle base; // Embed the Vehicle struct
    int num_doors;
} Car;

// Derived struct: Motorcycle (embedding Vehicle)
typedef struct Motorcycle {
    Vehicle base; // Embed the Vehicle struct
    int has_sidecar; // 1 for yes, 0 for no
} Motorcycle;

// Function to initialize a Vehicle
void initVehicle(Vehicle* v, const char* model, int engine_size) {
    strcpy(v->model, model);
    v->engine_size = engine_size;
}

// Function to initialize a Car
void initCar(Car* car, const char* model, int engine_size, int num_doors) {
    initVehicle(&car->base, model, engine_size); // Initialize the embedded Vehicle
part
    car->num_doors = num_doors;
}

// Function to initialize a Motorcycle
void initMotorcycle(Motorcycle* motorcycle, const char* model, int engine_size, int
has_sidecar) {
    initVehicle(&motorcycle->base, model, engine_size); // Initialize the embedded
Vehicle part
    motorcycle->has_sidecar = has_sidecar;
}

// Function to print Vehicle information
void printVehicleInfo(const Vehicle* v) {
    printf("Model: %s, Engine Size: %dcc\n", v->model, v->engine_size);
}

// Function to print Car information (extends Vehicle info)
void printCarInfo(const Car* car) {
    printf("Car - ");
    printVehicleInfo(&car->base); // Reuse Vehicle info printing
    printf("Number of Doors: %d\n", car->num_doors);
}

// Function to print Motorcycle information (extends Vehicle info)
void printMotorcycleInfo(const Motorcycle* motorcycle) {
    printf("Motorcycle - ");
```

```
    printVehicleInfo(&motorcycle->base); // Reuse Vehicle info printing
    printf("Has Sidecar: %s\n", motorcycle->has_sidecar ? "Yes" : "No");
}


int main() {
    Car myCar;
    initCar(&myCar, "Sedan X", 2000, 4);

    Motorcycle myMotorcycle;
    initMotorcycle(&myMotorcycle, "Cruiser 500", 500, 0);

    printCarInfo(&myCar);       // Output: Car - Model: Sedan X, Engine Size: 2000cc,
Number of Doors: 4
    printMotorcycleInfo(&myMotorcycle); // Output: Motorcycle - Model: Cruiser
500, Engine Size: 500cc, Has Sidecar: No

    return 0;
}
```

In this example, Car and Motorcycle structs *embed* the Vehicle struct as their base member. Initialization functions initCar and initMotorcycle first call initVehicle to initialize the embedded Vehicle part, effectively *reusing* the base initialization logic. printCarInfo and printMotorcycleInfo also reuse printVehicleInfo to display common vehicle information. This demonstrates a form of code reuse and hierarchical structuring reminiscent of inheritance. However, it is important to note that this is *composition*, not true inheritance. C does not have the same runtime type hierarchy or dynamic dispatch mechanisms as OOP languages. We are manually structuring our code to achieve similar organizational benefits. Accessing members of the embedded Vehicle struct within Car or Motorcycle is done through car->base.model, motorcycle->base.engine_size, etc. This explicit access to the embedded struct distinguishes it from true inheritance where derived class members directly inherit and access base class members without explicit qualification (Martin, 2008).

Polymorphism using function pointers is the key to achieving runtime flexibility and dynamic behavior in our OOP simulation in C. As seen in Chapter 14, function pointers allow us to associate different function implementations with different structure types. We can extend the inheritance example to incorporate polymorphic behavior. Let's add a startEngine operation to our Vehicle hierarchy, where the way an engine is started might differ between cars and motorcycles:

```
#include <stdio.h>
#include <stdlib.h>
#include <string.h>

// Base struct: Vehicle (with function pointer for polymorphic operation)
typedef struct Vehicle {
   char model[50];
   int engine_size;
   void (*startEngine)(struct Vehicle*); // Function pointer for startEngine
} Vehicle;

// Derived struct: Car (embedding Vehicle)
typedef struct Car {
   Vehicle base;
   int num_doors;
} Car;

// Derived struct: Motorcycle (embedding Vehicle)
typedef struct Motorcycle {
   Vehicle base;
   int has_sidecar;
} Motorcycle;

// Vehicle's default startEngine implementation (can be overridden in derived types)
void vehicleStartEngine(Vehicle* v) {
   printf("Generic Vehicle engine starting (Model: %s)...\n", v->model);
}

// Car's specific startEngine implementation (overrides Vehicle's)
void carStartEngine(Vehicle* v) { // Note: Parameter is still Vehicle*, but we'll treat
it as Car*
   Car* car = (Car*)v; // Cast to Car* to access Car-specific members (though not
used here in this simple example)
   printf("Car engine starting (Model: %s, Doors: %d)...\n", car->base.model, car-
>num_doors);
   printf("Ignition turned, starter motor engaged, engine roars to life!\n");
```

```
}

// Motorcycle's specific startEngine implementation (overrides Vehicle's)
void motorcycleStartEngine(Vehicle* v) { // Note: Parameter is still Vehicle*, but
we'll treat it as Motorcycle*
   Motorcycle* motorcycle = (Motorcycle*)v; // Cast to Motorcycle*
   printf("Motorcycle engine starting (Model: %s, Sidecar: %s)...\n", motorcycle-
>base.model, motorcycle->has_sidecar ? "Yes" : "No");
   printf("Kickstand up, throttle adjusted, engine purrs...\n");
}


// ... (initVehicle, initCar, initMotorcycle, printVehicleInfo, printCarInfo,
printMotorcycleInfo functions from previous example remain largely the same, but
init functions need to assign function pointers) ...

// Modified initCar to assign function pointer
void initCar(Car* car, const char* model, int engine_size, int num_doors) {
   initVehicle(&car->base, model, engine_size);
   car->base.startEngine = carStartEngine; // Assign Car-specific startEngine
function pointer
   car->num_doors = num_doors;
}

// Modified initMotorcycle to assign function pointer
void initMotorcycle(Motorcycle* motorcycle, const char* model, int engine_size, int
has_sidecar) {
   initVehicle(&motorcycle->base, model, engine_size);
   motorcycle->base.startEngine = motorcycleStartEngine; // Assign Motorcycle-
specific startEngine function pointer
   motorcycle->has_sidecar = has_sidecar;
}

// Modified initVehicle to assign default startEngine (for generic Vehicles - though
we mostly deal with Car/Motorcycle in this example)
void initVehicle(Vehicle* v, const char* model, int engine_size) {
   strcpy(v->model, model);
   v->engine_size = engine_size;
   v->startEngine = vehicleStartEngine; // Assign default startEngine function
pointer
}


int main() {
   Car myCar;
   initCar(&myCar, "Sedan X", 2000, 4);

   Motorcycle myMotorcycle;
   initMotorcycle(&myMotorcycle, "Cruiser 500", 500, 0);
```

```
    Vehicle* vehiclePtr1 = (Vehicle*)&myCar;    // Treat Car as a Vehicle (upcasting - implicit in C)
    Vehicle* vehiclePtr2 = (Vehicle*)&myMotorcycle; // Treat Motorcycle as a Vehicle (upcasting - implicit in C)

    printf("Starting vehicles...\n");
    vehiclePtr1->startEngine(vehiclePtr1); // Call startEngine through function pointer on Car object
    vehiclePtr2->startEngine(vehiclePtr2); // Call startEngine through function pointer on Motorcycle object

    // Output:
    // Starting vehicles...
    // Car engine starting (Model: Sedan X, Doors: 4)...
    // Ignition turned, starter motor engaged, engine roars to life!
    // Motorcycle engine starting (Model: Cruiser 500, Sidecar: No)...
    // Kickstand up, throttle adjusted, engine purrs...

    return 0;
}
```

In this enhanced example, the Vehicle struct now includes a function pointer startEngine. carStartEngine and motorcycleStartEngine are specific implementations for cars and motorcycles. In initCar and initMotorcycle, we *assign* these specific function implementations to the startEngine function pointer of the embedded Vehicle base struct. In main(), when we call vehiclePtr1->startEngine(vehiclePtr1) and vehiclePtr2->startEngine(vehiclePtr2), even though we are calling startEngine through a Vehicle* pointer, the *correct* function implementation (carStartEngine for myCar, motorcycleStartEngine for myMotorcycle) is executed due to the function pointer assignment during initialization. This demonstrates polymorphism – the same function call (startEngine) behaves differently based on the actual type of the object (Car or Motorcycle) at runtime, achieved through function pointers and struct composition. As Sommerville emphasizes in "Software Engineering" (Sommerville, 2011), polymorphism is crucial for creating flexible and extensible software systems, allowing for adding new types or behaviors without modifying existing code that interacts with the polymorphic interface.

Limitations and Considerations:

It's important to acknowledge the limitations of this OOP simulation in C compared to true OOP languages:

- **Manual Implementation:** OOP concepts are achieved through manual coding conventions and design patterns, not language enforcement. It requires more discipline and careful coding from the programmer.
- **Lack of Built-in Inheritance Hierarchy:** C doesn't have a built-in class hierarchy or automatic type checking for inheritance. Type relationships are managed through struct embedding and manual casting. Upcasting (treating a Car* as a Vehicle*) is generally implicit, but downcasting (treating a Vehicle* as a Car*) requires explicit casting and is less type-safe and requires careful management by the programmer to ensure type correctness.
- **No Automatic Dynamic Dispatch:** Polymorphism is achieved through explicit function pointer calls. C doesn't have automatic virtual function dispatch as in C++. You must explicitly call the function through the function pointer.
- **Memory Management:** Manual memory management in C remains crucial. You are responsible for allocating and freeing memory for structs and any dynamically allocated data members. Incorrect memory management can lead to memory leaks and errors, as with any C program.
- **Complexity for Complex Hierarchies:** While these techniques work well for relatively simple inheritance structures, managing very deep or complex inheritance

hierarchies in C using this simulation can become more intricate and harder to maintain compared to true OOP languages.

Despite these limitations, understanding how to simulate OOP principles in C is highly valuable. It allows C programmers to apply object-oriented design patterns where appropriate, enhancing code structure and maintainability, particularly in systems where performance and low-level control, strengths of C, are paramount, even if full-fledged OOP features are not available or desired.

In conclusion, while C is fundamentally procedural, techniques using structs and function pointers enable effective simulation of key object-oriented concepts like inheritance and polymorphism. Struct composition allows for creating inheritance-like relationships, promoting code reuse and hierarchical data organization. Function pointers are the cornerstone of polymorphism in C, enabling dynamic behavior and allowing code to operate on objects of different simulated types through a common interface. Mastering these techniques expands the C programmer's toolkit, allowing for more structured, flexible, and maintainable C code, drawing valuable principles from OOP design even within the procedural paradigm of C. This chapter has provided a foundation for understanding these OOP simulation techniques, and further exploration of design patterns in C, more complex inheritance models, and comparisons to true OOP languages can further deepen your understanding and application of these powerful concepts in C programming.

Chapter 17 Crafting Professional C Code

In this chapter, you will learn the following:

1. Code Optimization Techniques
2. Debugging and Error Handling
3. Security Considerations in C
4. Writing Efficient and Maintainable C Code

Optimization, Robustness, and Security

As we progress in our journey through C programming, moving beyond the fundamentals and data structures, we arrive at a critical juncture – the transition from writing code that simply *works* to writing code that is *professional.* Professional C code is characterized not only by its functional correctness but also by its efficiency, robustness, security, and maintainability. In real-world software development, especially in performance-sensitive domains like system programming, embedded systems, and high-performance computing where C often excels, these qualities are paramount. Imagine a server application handling thousands of requests per second; code optimization is crucial to ensure responsiveness and efficient resource utilization. Consider safety-critical embedded systems in automotive or aerospace industries; robust debugging and error handling are non-negotiable for reliability and safety. Reflect on the ever-increasing landscape of cyber threats; security considerations must be woven into the fabric of C code, especially when dealing with system-level operations or network-facing applications. This chapter delves into these essential aspects of professional C programming – code optimization techniques to enhance performance, debugging and error handling strategies to ensure robustness, security considerations to mitigate vulnerabilities, and principles for writing efficient and maintainable code, equipping learners with the skills and mindset to craft C programs that are not only functional but also high-quality, reliable, and secure.

Code Optimization Techniques are a vital aspect of software development, especially in performance-conscious domains where C is often chosen for its efficiency. The goal of code optimization is to improve the performance of a program, typically measured in terms of execution speed or resource consumption (memory, power). However, optimization should always be approached strategically and judiciously. Premature or misguided optimization can lead to code that is harder to understand, maintain, and even less performant in some cases (Knuth, 1974). A fundamental principle of optimization is *profiling first.* Before attempting any optimization, it's essential to *identify performance bottlenecks* – the parts of the code that consume the most execution time. Profiling tools (like gprof, perf, or profilers integrated into IDEs) help pinpoint these hotspots. Optimization efforts should then be focused on these critical sections of code, as optimizing non-bottleneck areas will yield negligible performance gains and potentially complicate the code unnecessarily. Optimization techniques can be broadly categorized:

- **Algorithm and Data Structure Selection:** Choosing the right algorithm and data structure is often the most impactful optimization strategy. For example, using a hash table for lookups instead of a linear search in a large dataset can dramatically improve performance from O(n) to near O(1). Similarly, using a more efficient sorting algorithm (like merge sort or quicksort) instead of bubble sort can be crucial for sorting large datasets (Sedgewick & Wayne, 2011). The choice should be driven by the specific performance characteristics of the problem and data size.
- **Compiler Optimization:** Modern C compilers are highly sophisticated and offer various optimization levels (e.g., -O1, -O2, -O3 in GCC and Clang, or /O1, /O2 in Visual Studio's compiler). These compiler optimizations perform a range of

transformations, such as inlining functions, loop unrolling, register allocation, and instruction scheduling, often significantly improving performance with minimal programmer effort. It is generally recommended to enable compiler optimizations in release builds. However, be aware that higher optimization levels might sometimes increase compilation time and, in rare cases, expose subtle bugs in the code or compiler itself.

- **Manual Micro-optimizations (Use with Caution):** These involve fine-tuning code at a lower level, often considering processor architecture and instruction sets. Examples include loop unrolling, reducing function call overhead (inlining, although compilers often do this automatically), minimizing memory accesses, and using bitwise operations instead of slower arithmetic operations where applicable. However, micro-optimizations should be applied sparingly and *only after profiling has identified them as critical bottlenecks* because they can often make code less readable and maintainable and might not be portable across different architectures or compiler versions. Furthermore, modern compilers are often better at micro-optimizing code than manual attempts in many scenarios.

Let's consider a practical example – optimizing string manipulation in C. Imagine you are frequently copying substrings within a larger text processing application. Using strcpy() repeatedly for substrings, especially if dealing with potentially overlapping memory regions, can be inefficient and potentially unsafe. Functions like strncpy() offer more control over the number of characters copied and can mitigate buffer overflow risks, but they still might not be the most performant for substring operations in all cases. For highly optimized substring operations, especially in performance-critical text processing, you might consider designing custom functions that leverage pointer arithmetic and memory manipulation directly, potentially using memcpy() for efficient block copying when appropriate and carefully managing null termination. However, before embarking on custom highly optimized string routines, it's crucial to *profile* to confirm that string manipulation is indeed a performance bottleneck and then *benchmark* your optimized routines against standard library functions to ensure actual performance gains. As Bentley advises in "Writing Efficient Programs" (Bentley, 1982), focus on clarity and correctness first, and optimize only when and where performance profiling demonstrates a genuine need, always measuring the impact of optimizations to ensure they are effective and do not introduce regressions or increase complexity unnecessarily.

Debugging and Error Handling are indispensable components of robust software development in C, a language known for its power and flexibility but also its potential for subtle errors, particularly related to memory management. Effective debugging is the process of identifying, locating, and fixing errors (bugs) in code. Robust error handling is about anticipating potential problems during program execution (e.g., invalid input, file access errors, memory allocation failures) and implementing mechanisms to gracefully handle these errors without crashing the program and, ideally, providing informative feedback to the user or logging system.

- **Debugging Tools and Techniques:** C programmers have a range of debugging tools at their disposal:
  - **Debuggers (e.g., GDB, LLDB, Visual Studio Debugger):** Interactive debuggers are powerful tools that allow you to step through code execution line by line, inspect variable values, set breakpoints, examine call stacks, and analyze memory. Mastering a debugger is essential for effective debugging in C. They enable you to understand the program's state at any point in execution and pinpoint the exact location and cause of errors.
  - **Print Statements (printf, fprintf for debugging output):** While often considered a more basic technique, strategically placed printf or fprintf statements can be surprisingly effective for quick debugging, especially for understanding program flow and inspecting intermediate values. Directing debugging output to stderr (using fprintf(stderr, ...) is good practice to separate it from normal program output. However, excessive use of print statements can clutter code and should be removed or conditionally compiled out (e.g., using #ifdef DEBUG ... #endif) in release builds.
  - **Assertions (assert.h):** Assertions are a powerful tool for catching programming errors early in the development process. assert(condition) checks if a condition is true at runtime. If the condition is false, the program terminates with an error message, indicating a programming mistake. Assertions should be used to check *preconditions*,

postconditions, and *invariants* – conditions that are expected to be true at certain points in the code if the program is working correctly. Assertions are typically enabled during development and testing and disabled in release builds (e.g., by defining NDEBUG).

- **Memory Checkers (e.g., Valgrind, AddressSanitizer):** Memory checkers are invaluable for detecting memory-related errors in C, such as memory leaks, buffer overflows, use-after-free errors, and invalid memory accesses. Tools like Valgrind (for Linux) and AddressSanitizer (part of compilers like Clang and GCC) run your program and monitor memory operations, reporting errors when they are detected. Using memory checkers is crucial for ensuring memory safety in C programs, especially those using dynamic memory allocation.
- **Static Analysis Tools (e.g., Clang Static Analyzer, Cppcheck):** Static analysis tools examine source code without executing it, looking for potential errors, style violations, and security vulnerabilities. They can identify issues like potential null pointer dereferences, buffer overflows, format string bugs, and code style inconsistencies. Incorporating static analysis into your development workflow can help catch errors early, before runtime, improving code quality and reducing debugging effort.

- **Error Handling Strategies:** Robust error handling is crucial for preventing program crashes and ensuring graceful degradation in the face of errors. Common strategies include:
  - **Return Codes:** Functions can return error codes to signal success or failure and provide information about the error. Conventionally, 0 or a positive value indicates success, and a negative value or a specific error code (often defined as macros) indicates an error. The calling function is then responsible for checking the return code and handling the error appropriately. Functions like fopen(), malloc(), and many system calls in C return error codes.
  - **Error Messages (using perror, fprintf(stderr, ...)):** When an error occurs, providing informative error messages is crucial for debugging and user feedback. perror(string) (from <stdio.h>) prints a user-supplied string followed by a system error message describing the last error. fprintf(stderr, ...) can be used to print custom error messages to the standard error stream (stderr), which is typically directed to the console or log files, separating error output from normal program output.
  - **Assertions (for detecting programmer errors during development):** As discussed earlier, assert() is for detecting *programming errors* that should *never* occur in a correct program. They are not intended for handling runtime errors like invalid user input or file access failures. Assertions are for development-time checks, not

runtime error handling in production code.

- **Exception-like Handling (using setjmp/longjmp - use cautiously):** C provides setjmp() and longjmp() (from <setjmp.h>) which can be used to implement a form of non-local control flow, similar to exceptions in other languages. setjmp() saves the current program context, and longjmp() jumps back to a previously saved context. While they can be used for error handling, setjmp/longjmp should be used *very cautiously* as they can make code harder to understand and maintain, disrupt normal program flow, and potentially lead to resource leaks if not used very carefully (Lakos, 1996). For most common error handling scenarios in C, return codes, error messages, and assertions are usually sufficient and preferred over setjmp/longjmp due to their better maintainability and predictability.

Let's illustrate debugging and error handling with an example that involves dynamic memory allocation and file I/O:

```
#include <stdio.h>
#include <stdlib.h>
#include <string.h>
#include <errno.h>
#include <assert.h> // For assert

int main() {
    FILE *fptr = NULL;
    char filename[] = "my_important_data.txt";
    int *data_buffer = NULL;
    size_t num_elements = 10;

    // Attempt to open file for writing
    fptr = fopen(filename, "w");
    if (fptr == NULL) {
```

```
        perror("Error opening file for writing"); // Error message using perror
        return 1; // Return error code
    }

    // Allocate memory for data buffer
    data_buffer = (int *)malloc(num_elements * sizeof(int));
    if (data_buffer == NULL) {
        fprintf(stderr, "Memory allocation failed!\n"); // Error message to stderr
        fclose(fptr); // Important: Close file even if memory allocation fails
        return 1; // Return error code
    }
    assert(data_buffer != NULL); // Assertion - should not reach here if malloc fails as
we already handled NULL case

    // ... (Simulate some data writing - let's just write some numbers for example) ...
    for (size_t i = 0; i < num_elements; i++) {
        fprintf(fptr, "%d\n", (int)i * 10);
    }


    // Attempt to close file
    if (fclose(fptr) != 0) { // Check return code of fclose
        perror("Error closing file"); // Error message if closing fails
        free(data_buffer); // Still need to free allocated memory even if file closing fails.
        return 1;
    }
    fptr = NULL; // Good practice to set pointer to NULL after closing

    printf("Data written to file '%s' successfully.\n", filename);


    // ... (Later in the program, perhaps read and process the data - not implemented
here for brevity) ...


    free(data_buffer); // Free dynamically allocated memory
    data_buffer = NULL; // Good practice to set pointer to NULL after freeing

    return 0; // Success
}
```

This example demonstrates error handling for file opening, memory allocation, and file closing using return codes, error messages (using perror and fprintf(stderr, ...)), and an assertion (although the assertion is technically redundant here as we already handled the malloc NULL case, it shows how assertions can be used to enforce expected conditions). In a real debugging scenario, if you suspect a memory leak, you could run this program under Valgrind or AddressSanitizer to detect potential leaks. If you are experiencing unexpected program behavior, you could use a debugger to step through the code, inspect variables, and identify the root cause.

Security Considerations in C are of paramount importance, especially as C is often used for system-level programming and applications that handle sensitive data or interact with networks. C's low-level nature and manual memory management, while providing power and flexibility, also make it prone to certain types of security vulnerabilities if not programmed carefully (Howard & LeBlanc, 2003). Common security vulnerabilities in C programs include:

- **Buffer Overflows:** Occur when data is written beyond the allocated bounds of a buffer (e.g., character array, dynamically allocated memory). Buffer overflows can overwrite adjacent memory regions, potentially corrupting data, crashing the program, or, more critically, allowing attackers to inject malicious code and take control of the system. Buffer overflows are often exploited in stack-based and heap-based buffer overflows.
- **Format String Vulnerabilities:** Arise from improper use of format string functions like printf, fprintf, sprintf, and scanf when the format string itself comes from external, untrusted input (e.g., user input, network data). Attackers can craft malicious format strings to read from or write to arbitrary memory locations, potentially gaining control of the program or leaking sensitive information.

- **Integer Overflows:** Occur when the result of an integer arithmetic operation exceeds the maximum value that the integer data type can hold. Integer overflows can lead to unexpected behavior, incorrect calculations, and in some cases, can be exploited for security vulnerabilities, particularly when overflowed values are used for buffer sizes or memory allocation sizes.
- **Dangling Pointers and Use-After-Free:** Dangling pointers are pointers that point to memory that has been freed or is no longer valid. Use-after-free vulnerabilities occur when a program attempts to dereference a dangling pointer. These errors can lead to crashes, unpredictable behavior, and potential security exploits if freed memory is reallocated and contains sensitive data.
- **Race Conditions (in multithreaded programs):** Race conditions occur in multithreaded programs when the order of execution of threads can lead to unexpected or incorrect results, especially when multiple threads access shared resources (memory, files) without proper synchronization mechanisms (locks, mutexes, semaphores). Race conditions can be difficult to debug and can lead to data corruption, program errors, and security vulnerabilities.

Solutions and Best Practices for Security in C:

- **Input Validation:** Thoroughly validate all external input (user input, network data, data from files) to ensure it conforms to expected formats, lengths, and ranges before processing it. Input validation helps prevent buffer overflows, format string vulnerabilities, and other input-related issues. For strings, check lengths and character types. For numerical input, check ranges and data types.
- **Bounds Checking:** Always perform bounds checking when accessing arrays or buffers to prevent buffer overflows. Use functions like strncpy and strncat instead of strcpy and strcat to limit the number of characters copied, and always check buffer sizes before writing to them.
- **Safe String Functions:** Prefer safer string handling functions like strncpy, strncat, snprintf over potentially unsafe functions like strcpy, strcat, sprintf. These "n" versions allow you to specify buffer sizes, reducing buffer overflow risks.
- **Memory Safety Tools:** Utilize memory safety tools like Valgrind and AddressSanitizer during development and testing to detect memory leaks, buffer overflows, and other memory-related errors early. AddressSanitizer, in particular, is excellent for catching buffer overflows at runtime.
- **Address Space Layout Randomization (ASLR) and Data Execution Prevention (DEP):** These operating system-level security features help mitigate some types of buffer overflow exploits. Ensure that these features are enabled in your

development and deployment environments. Compilers and linkers also often provide options to enable security features like stack canaries, which can detect stack buffer overflows at runtime.

- **Secure Coding Guidelines:** Adhere to secure coding guidelines and best practices specific to C programming. Organizations like CERT (Computer Emergency Response Team) and OWASP (Open Web Application Security Project) provide valuable secure coding guidelines for C and C++. These guidelines cover various aspects of secure coding, including input validation, memory management, error handling, and common vulnerability prevention.
- **Regular Security Audits and Code Reviews:** Conduct regular security audits and code reviews, especially for security-sensitive code. Security audits can help identify potential vulnerabilities, and code reviews can help catch coding errors and security flaws early in the development cycle.

Let's illustrate input validation to prevent a potential buffer overflow in a string copy scenario:

```
#include <stdio.h>
#include <stdlib.h>
#include <string.h>

int main() {
   char source_string[] = "This is a potentially very long string that might exceed the
destination buffer size.";
   char destination_buffer[50]; // Destination buffer of size 50

   // Vulnerable code (potential buffer overflow):
```

```
    // strcpy(destination_buffer, source_string); // If source_string is longer than 49,
buffer overflow!

    // Secure code with bounds checking and strncpy:
    size_t dest_buffer_size = sizeof(destination_buffer);
    strncpy(destination_buffer, source_string, dest_buffer_size - 1); // Copy at most
dest_buffer_size - 1 bytes
    destination_buffer[dest_buffer_size - 1] = '\0'; // Ensure null termination
(important for strncpy)

    printf("Copied string: %s\n", destination_buffer); // Output: Copied string: This
is a potentially very long string that m

    return 0;
}
```

In this example, strncpy is used instead of strcpy to limit the number of characters copied to prevent a buffer overflow if source_string is longer than destination_buffer. Crucially, we also explicitly null-terminate destination_buffer after strncpy because strncpy might not null-terminate if the source string is longer than or equal to the specified size limit. This demonstrates a basic, but important, security practice – bounds checking and using safer alternatives to potentially unsafe functions. As Seacord details in "Secure Coding in C and C++" (Seacord, 2013), adopting secure coding practices proactively throughout the development lifecycle is essential for mitigating security risks in C programs.

Writing Efficient and Maintainable C Code is the hallmark of professional software engineering. Efficiency and maintainability are not mutually exclusive but rather synergistic qualities. Code that is well-structured, readable, and modular is often easier to optimize, debug, and maintain over the long term. Conversely, code that is overly complex, poorly formatted, and lacks clear structure becomes a maintenance nightmare, consuming significant development time and resources, even if it might be micro-optimized in certain areas.

Principles for Efficient and Maintainable C Code:

- **Code Style and Formatting:** Adopt a consistent coding style and formatting convention (e.g., K&R style, Google C++ Style Guide, GNU Coding Standards). Consistent formatting improves readability and makes it easier to understand the code's structure and logic. Use tools like indent or clang-format to automatically format code consistently.
- **Comments and Documentation:** Write clear and concise comments to explain complex logic, non-obvious code sections, and the purpose of functions and data structures. Document function interfaces (purpose, parameters, return values, preconditions, postconditions). Use documentation generators (like Doxygen) to create structured documentation from code comments. Well-documented code is easier for others (and your future self) to understand and maintain.
- **Modularity (Functions and Files):** Break down large programs into smaller, self-contained modules (functions and files). Each function should have a clear, well-defined purpose and perform a single logical task. Organize code into files based on logical modules or functionalities. Modularity improves code organization, reusability, testability, and maintainability. Strive for functions with low coupling and high cohesion (high cohesion within a module, low coupling between modules).
- **Meaningful Variable and Function Names:** Choose descriptive and meaningful names for variables and functions that clearly indicate their purpose. Avoid cryptic abbreviations or

single-letter variable names (except for common loop counters like i, j, k). Well-chosen names significantly enhance code readability and understanding.

- **Avoid Global Variables (Minimize Scope):** Minimize the use of global variables. Global variables can make code harder to reason about, debug, and maintain, as they can be modified from anywhere in the program, increasing coupling and reducing modularity. Prefer passing data explicitly as function parameters and limiting variable scope to the smallest necessary region (local variables whenever possible).
- **Use const Where Appropriate:** Use the const keyword to declare variables and function parameters that should not be modified. const provides compile-time type safety and improves code readability by clearly indicating intent. It also helps compilers perform optimizations and can catch accidental modifications of read-only data.
- **Assertions (for development-time code validation):** As discussed earlier, use assertions to check preconditions, postconditions, and invariants during development and testing to catch programming errors early.
- **Code Reviews:** Conduct code reviews regularly, especially for critical code sections. Code reviews by peers can help identify errors, improve code quality, enforce coding standards, and promote knowledge sharing within a team.
- **Testing (Unit Testing, Integration Testing):** Implement thorough testing, including unit tests (testing individual functions or modules in isolation) and integration tests (testing interactions

between modules). Automated testing frameworks (like Check or CUnit) can streamline the testing process and ensure code quality and robustness.

Let's illustrate code maintainability by refactoring a piece of hypothetical less maintainable code:

Less Maintainable Code (Hypothetical Example):

```
// Hypothetical less maintainable code - hard to read, understand, and modify
int process_data(int type, int value, char* str, int len) {
    if (type == 1) {
        if (value > 100) {
            if (len > 0) {
                // ... complex logic using value, str, and len ...
                return 1;
            } else {
                return -1;
            }
        } else {
            // ... another complex logic based on value and type ...
            return 2;
        }
    } else if (type == 2) {
        // ... completely different logic for type 2 ...
        return 3;
    } else {
        return -2; // Invalid type
    }
    return 0; // Should not reach here in theory but needed to avoid compiler warning
}
```

Refactored More Maintainable Code:

C

```
// More maintainable code - broken down into smaller functions, clearer logic,
comments
// Function to handle data processing for type 1 and value > 100
static int process_type1_high_value(int value, char* str, int len) {
    if (len <= 0) {
        return -1; // Error: Invalid length
```

```
    }
    // ... complex logic using value, str, and len (now in a dedicated function) ...
    // ... comments explaining the logic ...
    return 1; // Success for type 1, high value case
}

// Function to handle data processing for type 1 and value <= 100
static int process_type1_low_value(int value) {
    // ... another complex logic based on value and type (now in a dedicated function)
...
    // ... comments explaining the logic ...
    return 2; // Success for type 1, low value case
}

// Function to handle data processing for type 2
static int process_type2_data(int value, char* str, int len) { // Added parameters if
needed for type 2 later, even if not used now.
    // ... completely different logic for type 2 (now in a dedicated function) ...
    // ... comments explaining the logic ...
    return 3; // Success for type 2 case
}


// Main processing function - now much cleaner and easier to understand
int process_data(int type, int value, char* str, int len) {
    if (type == 1) {
        if (value > 100) {
            return process_type1_high_value(value, str, len); // Call dedicated function
        } else {
            return process_type1_low_value(value);       // Call dedicated function
        }
    } else if (type == 2) {
        return process_type2_data(value, str, len);      // Call dedicated function
    } else {
        return -2; // Error: Invalid type
    }
    return 0; // Should not reach here in theory - but kept for completeness. Consider
assert(0) or removing it after more robust type handling.
}
```

The refactored code is more maintainable due to: decomposition into smaller, more focused functions (process_type1_high_value, process_type1_low_value, process_type2_data), clearer function names, potential for adding comments within each smaller function to explain specific logic, and reduced nesting and complexity within the main process_data function, making it easier to understand and modify individual processing logic for different types without impacting other parts of the code. As Hunt and Thomas argue in "The Pragmatic Programmer" (Hunt & Thomas, 1999), writing clean, well-structured code is an investment that pays off significantly in reduced debugging time, easier maintenance, and increased overall software development efficiency over the long term.

In conclusion, mastering code optimization, debugging and error handling, security considerations, and writing efficient and maintainable C code are essential for transitioning from writing functional C code to crafting professional-quality C software. These skills are not merely about technical proficiency in C syntax; they are about adopting a professional mindset, embracing best practices, and continuously striving to improve the quality, reliability, and security of your C programs. This chapter has provided a foundation for these crucial aspects of professional C programming, and continuous learning, practice, and adherence to established software engineering principles will further solidify these skills, enabling you to build robust, efficient, secure, and maintainable C applications across diverse domains.

Bibliography

1. Anderson, G. (2006). Foundations of Multithreaded, Parallel, and Distributed Programming. Addison-Wesley Professional.
2. Banahan, M., Brady, D., & Doran, M. (1991). The C book. Addison-Wesley.
3. Barr, M. (2015). Programming embedded systems: With C and GNU development tools. Newnes.
4. Bentley, J. L. (1982). Writing efficient programs. Prentice-Hall, Inc.
5. Cormen, T. H., Leiserson, C. E., Rivest, R. L., & Stein, C. (2009). Introduction to algorithms. MIT press.
6. Deitel, P. J., & Deitel, H. M. (2015). C: How to program. Pearson Education.
7. Gamma, E., Helm, R., Johnson, R., & Vlissides, J. (1994). Design patterns: Elements of reusable object-oriented software. Addison-Wesley Professional.
8. Hanly, J. R., & Koffman, E. B. (2009). Problem solving and program design in C. Pearson Education.
9. Harbison, S. P., & Steele Jr, G. L. (2002). C: A reference manual. Prentice Hall.
10. Howard, M., & LeBlanc, D. (2003). Writing secure code. Microsoft Press.
11. Hunt, A., & Thomas, D. (1999). The pragmatic programmer: From journeyman to master. Addison-Wesley Professional.
12. Kernighan, B. W., & Ritchie, D. M. (1988). The C programming language. Prentice Hall.
13. King, K. N. (2008). C programming: A modern approach. W. W. Norton & Company.
14. Knuth, D. E. (1974). Structured programming with go to statements. ACM Computing Surveys (CSUR), 6(4), 261-301.
15. Knuth, D. E. (1998). The art of computer programming, volume 3: sorting and searching. Addison-Wesley Professional.
16. Koenig, A. (1994). C traps and pitfalls. ACM SIGPLAN Notices, 29(1), 35-40.
17. Lakos, J. O. (1996). Large-scale C++ software design. Addison-Wesley Professional.
18. Liskov, B., & Guttag, J. (2001). Program development in Java: Abstraction,

specification, and object-oriented design. Addison-Wesley Professional.

19. Maguire, S. (1993). Writing solid code: Microsoft's techniques for developing bug-free C programs. Microsoft Press.
20. Martin, R. C. (2008). Clean code: A handbook of agile software craftsmanship. Prentice Hall.
21. McConnell, S. (2004). Code complete: A practical handbook of software construction. Microsoft Press.
22. Oualline, S. (1992). Practical C programming. O'Reilly Media, Inc.
23. Petzold, C. (1998). Programming Windows (5th ed.). Microsoft Press. (A classic and comprehensive guide to Windows API programming.)
24. Plauger, P. J. (1992). The standard C library. Prentice Hall.
25. Prata, S. (2014). C primer plus. Addison-Wesley Professional.
26. Puntambekar, A. A. (2008). Data types and modifiers in C. International Journal of Computer Science and Network Security, 8(7), 229-232.
27. Ritchie, D. M. (1993). The development of the C language. ACM SIGPLAN Notices, 28(3), 201-208.
28. Roberts, E. S. (1986). Thinking recursively. John Wiley & Sons, Inc.
29. Schildt, H. (2000). C: The complete reference. McGraw-Hill Education.
30. Seacord, R. C. (2013). Secure coding in C and C++. Addison-Wesley Professional.
31. Sedgewick, R., & Wayne, K. (2011). Algorithms. Addison-Wesley Professional.
32. Sommerville, I. (2011). Software engineering. Pearson Education.
33. Stevens, W. R. (2005). Advanced programming in the UNIX environment. Addison-Wesley Professional.
34. Tanenbaum, A. S., Augenstein, M. J., & Langsam, Y. (1990). Data structures using C. Prentice Hall.
35. Tanenbaum, A. S., & Woodhull, A. S. (2006). Operating systems: design and implementation. Pearson Prentice Hall.
36. Tondo, C. L., & Gimpel, S. L. (1994). The C programming language: structures, pointers, and functions. Prentice Hall.
37. Yourdon, E., & Constantine, L. L. (1979). Structured design: Fundamentals of a discipline of computer program and systems design. Prentice Hall.

About The Author

Early Life and Education

Mark John Lado was born on September 24, 1992, in Danao City, Philippines. From an early age, he exhibited a keen interest in technology and education, which would later shape his career. He pursued his Bachelor of Science in Information Systems (BSIS) at Colegio de San Antonio de Padua, where he graduated with a strong foundation in technology and systems analysis. His academic journey continued as he earned a Master's degree in Information Technology (MIT) from the Northern Negros State College of Science and Technology in Sagay City, Philippines. Currently, he is pursuing his Doctorate in Information Technology at the State University of Northern Negros, reflecting his commitment to lifelong learning and professional growth.

Professional Career

Mark has built a diverse and impactful career in education and technology. He currently serves as an Instructor in the College of Technology and Engineering at Cebu Technological University, a role he has held since October 2022. Prior to this, he was a Faculty member in Business Education and Information Systems at Colegio de San Antonio de Padua from 2018 to 2022. His earlier roles include working as a Part-Time Information Technology Instructor at the University of the Visayas

- Danao Branch and as an ICT Coordinator at Carmen Christian School Inc. in 2017.

Research and Innovation

Mark is an active researcher with a focus on applying technology to solve real-world problems. Some of his notable projects include:

1. "Development of a Microprocessor-Based Sensor Network for Monitoring Water Parameters in Tilapia Traponds"
2. "A Wireless Digital Public Address with Voice Alarm and Text-to-Speech Feature for Different Campuses", which was published in Globus: An International Journal of Management & IT

His research contributions highlight his dedication to innovation and his ability to bridge theoretical knowledge with practical applications.

Authorship and Publications

Mark is a prolific author, having written and published multiple books on technology topics. His works include:

1. Mastering CRUD with Flask in 5 Days; Build Python Web Applications - From Novice to...
2. Flask, PostgreSQL, and Bootstrap: Building Data-Driven Web Applications with CRUD...
3. From Model to Web App: A Comprehensive Guide to Building Data-Driven Web...
4. The Beginner's Guide Computer Systems; Principles, Practices, and Troubleshooting:...
5. Flask Web Framework Building Interactive Web Applications

with SQLite Database: A...

6. Mastering PC Troubleshooting & Operating Systems: The Modern Landscape of PC...
7. Mastering Flask in 5 Days; From Zero to Deployment: Building Your First Web App:...
8. Data Modeling and Process Analysis; Essential for Technology Analysts and AI...
9. The Echo of the Past; Information Networks from Stone to Silicon and Beyond AI: How...
10. Cybersecurity Essentials Protecting Your Digital Life, Data, and Privacy in a...
11. Mastering PC Troubleshooting and Operating Systems: The Future-Ready...
12. From Idea to Manuscript: A Step-by-Step Guide to Writing Your Nonfiction Book
13. Microprocessor Magic: Unlocking the Potential of Building Projects from Scratch
14. Data Modeling and Process Analysis: A Comprehensive Guide – Volume I
15. Python Data Science Essentials: A Comprehensive Guide to Mastering...
16. Mastering PC Troubleshooting and Operating Systems: A Comprehensive Guide
17. Cybersecurity Confidence: 8 Steps to Master Digital Security and Boost Productivity
18. Embedded Systems: From Historical Development to Modern-Day Applications

These books are widely recognized and serve as valuable resources for students, hobbyists, and professionals in the IT field. His publications are available on platforms like Amazon and ThriftBooks, further extending his reach and impact

Certifications and Professional Development

Mark has pursued several certifications to enhance his expertise, including:

- Computer Hardware Servicing from Cebu Technological University
- Consumer Electronics Servicing from TESDA

These certifications underscore his commitment to continuous professional development and staying updated with emerging technological trends.

Contributions to IT Education

As an active member of the Philippine Society of Information Technology Educators (PSITE), Mark contributes to advancing IT education standards in the Philippines. His teaching, research, and authorship have made him a respected figure in the academic and IT communities. He is known for his adaptability to emerging technologies, such as AI-driven systems and cybersecurity, ensuring that his work remains relevant and impactful.

Personal Interests

Outside of his professional life, Mark enjoys reading books, spending time at the beach, and engaging in physical activities like inline skating and biking. These hobbies not only help him unwind but also contribute to his overall well-being and creativity.

Legacy and Impact

Mark John Lado's dedication to education, research, and professional excellence has made him a valuable asset to the IT community. His contributions have empowered countless students and professionals, preparing them for the challenges of a rapidly evolving technological landscape. His unwavering passion for technology and continuous pursuit of learning ensure that his legacy will endure for years to come.

For more details about his work, you can visit his official website https://markjohnlado.com/

or explore his publications on Amazon Author Page

https://www.amazon.com/stores/author/B0BZM8PM6R

© 2025 Mark John Lado

I highly recommend reading this book to further enhance your skills and deepen your understanding of the subject.

https://a.co/d/ahv6VWa

https://a.co/d/b1W3F8n

https://a.co/d/izTWNbO

https://a.co/d/6HHyUFk

www.ingramcontent.com/pod-product-compliance
Lightning Source LLC
LaVergne TN
LVHW022345060326
832902LV00022B/4249

* 9 7 9 8 3 1 1 0 9 9 9 4 3 *